P9-ELG-275

3 1404 00740 8542

WITHDRAWN

MAY 0 6 2024

DAVID O. McKAY LIBRARY
BYU-IDAHO

APR 17 2003

PROPERTY OF:
DAVID O. McKAY LIBRARY
BYU-IDAHO
REXBURG ID 83460-0405

Understanding School Assessment

*A Parent and Community Guide
to Helping Students Learn*

Understanding School Assessment

A Parent and Community Guide
to Helping Students Learn

Jan Chappuis
and Stephen Chappuis

Assessment Training Institute • 317 SW Alder Street, Suite 1200 • Portland, OR 97204
www.assessmentinst.com

Project Coordinator: Barbara Carnegie

Editing: Robert L. Marcum

Design and Layout: Heidi Bay

Cover Design: Brass Design

To order, call 1-800-480-3060. A free discussion guide for study groups also is available.

© Copyright 2002

Assessment Training Institute, Inc., Portland, Oregon

All rights reserved. No part of this book may be reproduced or transmitted in any form or by any means, electronic or mechanical, including photocopy, recording, or any information storage and retrieval system, without permission in writing from the Assessment Training Institute, 317 SW Alder Street, Suite 1200, Portland, Oregon 97204.

Portions of this book are reprinted from "Classroom Assessment for Learning," by Stephen Chappuis and Richard J. Stiggins, *Educational Leadership*, *60*(1), 40–44. Copyright © 2002 by the Association for Supervision and Curriculum Development. Reprinted with permission from ASCD. All rights reserved.

2002 First Printing

Printed in the U.S.A.

ISBN 0-9655101-3-1

Library of Congress Control Number: 2002105512

Foreword

On the surface, it would appear that the most important assessments in schools are the annual standardized tests. After all, they command the attention of the president of the United States, who demands more of them to be sure "no child is left behind." They receive major attention in news reports, whether local, state, national, or international test scores. They command an investment of tens of millions of dollars annually as communities across the nation hold schools accountable for student learning. But the fact is that these politically important tests pale in their contribution to school success when compared to the assessments teachers develop, administer, and use day to day in the classroom. Given the decisions influenced by classroom assessments, it is not an overstatement to contend that a child's academic well-being hinges on the quality of these assessments and on the manner in which they are used.

In this parent and community guide to assessment in schools, Jan and Steve Chappuis explain why classroom assessment is so crucial to student well-being. They do so to explain the role of parents and the community in protecting that well-being. If classroom assessments are of inferior quality or are poorly used, students are placed directly in harm's way. The consequences for them and their learning can be painful and long lasting. But if classroom assessments are of high quality and are used well, students can soar to new heights of academic success. Again, Steve and Jan explain why.

Theirs are the voices of experience; they are uniquely qualified to address assessment issues in this context. They are parents raising a 9-year-old daughter, as well as specialists in professional development in the field of educational assessment. Both have years of experience in addressing school and community concerns around educational issues such as assessment. Few others are able to blend the caring sensitivity of parents with technical expertise and a background in community relations to provide practical insights that help parents and community act in the best interest of students.

As you read, I recommend that you tune into three specific aspects of the Chappuis' presentation.

The first and most important is their discussion of *the relationship between assessment and student motivation*. In effect, Jan and Steve show us how research on effective instruction, student learning, and achievement motivation over the past decade has redefined that relationship. The results reveal patterns of assessment use in the classroom that have proven immensely effective in "leaving no child behind." They recommend the use of classroom assessment not merely to check for learning or to assign report card grades, but to foster higher levels of achievement. They reveal the secrets of using assessment and its results to increase student confidence, so that students will continue to risk trying to learn. Because confident persistence is the key to any child's success in school, I believe you will find this part of the Chappuis' message intriguing.

Second, Steve and Jan list all of the *critically important decision makers*—the assessment users who rely on information about student achievement to do their jobs. They identify policy-level users, users who serve to support teachers (guidance personnel, special education staff, etc.), and classroom-level users. It is in this latter category where the startling new insight arises. The key assessment users in the classroom here are teachers, parents, and students—yes, students. We don't often think of students as decision makers who rely on assessment results to inform their actions. But Jan and Steve show us why their decisions turn out to be the most important of any. I am quite certain that you will be fascinated by their treatment of the student's role.

Third, the authors *frame parents' and the community's role in assessment.* Here they ask for an alliance unlike anything proposed before. Because of the power that assessment, evaluation, and grading practices exert in the classroom and school, they recommend that parents and members of the community at large ask questions about those practices. As it turns out, professional educators typically have not been given the opportunity to learn to address assessment issues productively. This is precisely why Jan, Steve, and all of us at the Assessment Training Institute are so concerned with student well-being. The assessments used with your child may fall short of standards of quality or might be poorly used. The only way to prevent that is to be sure that teachers and school leaders in your community have the opportunity to develop the expertise needed to avoid problems and promote maximum student success. This guide recommends concrete actions that parents and community members can take to ensure they have that opportunity.

As you will see on reading Jan and Steve's work, when that foundation of "assessment literacy" is in place, students learn a lot more and feel in control of their success—both keys to helping all students fulfill their individual academic potential. They seek your help as parents and community leaders in making that possible.

Rick Stiggins, president
Assessment Training Institute
Portland, Oregon

Acknowledgements

We would like to thank the countless students and educators with whom we've worked over the years and from whom we've learned valuable lessons about what's important in teaching and learning. We're especially grateful to the following teachers, administrators, and parents who shared with us topics they thought we should address: Linda Elman, Ron Engelland, Ken Hermann, David McVicker, Joan Moser, Corinne Pflug-Tilton, Claudia Rengstorf, Claudia Thompson, Shannon Thompson, Debbie Wing, Chris Wyatt, and Susan Zoller. Many of their suggestions helped frame the outline of this book.

We also express our appreciation to the Site Council at Mt. Tabor Middle School in Portland, Oregon, for their thoughtful feedback on our rough draft.

Our gratitude also goes to our coworkers at the Assessment Training Institute who helped in content and style, provided encouragement and support, and let us close our doors to work undisturbed: Judy Arter, Barbara Carnegie, Molly Grignon, Sharon Lippert, and Stacey Roy. We offer our special thanks to Rick Stiggins for so willingly sharing his personal vision, wisdom, and guidance.

Credit for increased clarity in our thoughts and words goes to our editor, freelancer Robert L. Marcum, and his purple pencil.

And finally, we are indebted to our daughter Claire for offering her insights into school, for causing us to see school through parents' eyes, and for enduring endless summer day camps as we finished this book.

Table of Contents

INTRODUCTION 1

CHAPTER 1
Assessment in School Today 5

What Is Assessment and Why Is It Changing? 5
What Is the Purpose of Assessment? 8
Who Needs Assessment Information? 9
Summative and Formative Decisions 13
Different Decisions, Different Assessments 20
Testing for Accountability 21
Assessment Literacy in the Schools 23
Important Ideas 25

CHAPTER 2
Connecting Student Motivation and Assessment 27

How Does Motivation Work? 27
Assessment as a Motivator in School 28
Research on Assessment, Motivation, and Student Achievement 30
Accurate Classroom Assessments 32
Descriptive Feedback 32
Student Involvement in Assessment 36
Important Ideas 41

CHAPTER 3

What Students Learn: Standards, Curriculum, and
Learning Targets 43

What Is a Curriculum?...45

What's Different About Curriculum Today? 46

Classroom Learning Targets: Four Categories 47

Who Benefits When Curriculum Is Defined? 52

How Parents Can Learn About the Written Curriculum 58

The Difficulties and Challenges Ahead 61

Important Ideas..63

CHAPTER 4

Classroom Assessment: Principles, Methods, and Issues
of Quality 65

Assessment Principles: Standards of Quality 66

Methods of Assessment..70

Which Method Is Best?..76

Issues of Quality..78

Formative Assessment and Student Involvement Within
Each Assessment Method..83

Helping with Homework 85

Important Ideas..91

CHAPTER 5

Standardized Testing 93

What Is a Standardized Test? 95

Using Standardized Tests When the Stakes Are High 104

Important Ideas..107

CHAPTER 6
Communicating About Student Learning 109

The Primary Purpose 110

What's in a Grade? 110

Beyond Letter Grades and Symbols............................... 116

Students as Communicators 118

Communication About Standardized Tests 120

Reconciling State Test Results to Report Card Grades 123

Important Ideas.. 126

CHAPTER 7
Putting the Pieces Together: Parent and Community Involvement in School Assessment.................................... 127

Working with the Schools.. 129

What Parents Should Know and Can Do 130

Conclusion.. 144

GLOSSARY OF ASSESSMENT TERMS 149

BIBLIOGRAPHY 155

Introduction

We have written this book as parents, intensely interested and actively involved in our daughter's learning. We also have written it as educators with a lifelong investment in teaching both children and adults, believing strongly in the power of classroom assessment to improve student learning. We have written this book as community members, interested in contributing to the success of our local schools and the improvement of public education in general.

We have written this book for parents, educators, and community members with the goal of increasing understanding about assessment in schools, and more specifically about the important role classroom assessment can play in school improvement. Parents and the broader community constitute the largest audience for assessment results, and as such, we believe the information you receive ought to be clear and understandable. Beyond that, we want to prepare you to be critical consumers of assessment results. To that end, our purpose is to share what we think parents and community members ought to know about assessment practices that will maximize student success in school. We think some readers may find what we have to report a bit surprising.

The Chapters Ahead

In the chapters that follow we describe what we believe are the assessment issues most important to understand if we, as a community, are to help improve our schools. Our ultimate goal is to help you identify assessment practices that contribute to

1

student failure and that potentially harm learners, and to show you other assessment practices that contribute to success and improve learning. To that end, we have structured each of the chapters around a set of guiding questions.

What is assessment? How has assessment changed since we were in school? Who are the key users of assessment information? What are the differences between assessment *of* learning and assessment *for* learning? In Chapter 1 we describe today's assessment landscape and discuss how its changing face affects students of today and tomorrow.

What assessment practices are likely to increase student motivation to learn? What role can assessment *for* learning play to support underachieving students? In Chapter 2 we explore the relationship between motivation and assessment. We look at what research tells us about connecting motivation and assessment in productive ways for *all* students.

Is there a high-quality written curriculum in place for each grade level and subject in my neighborhood schools? Is my child getting a clear picture of what she or he is to learn in school? How would I as a parent know that? Chapter 3 offers an explanation of the kinds of learning goals schools have and practices that make those goals clear to students.

What should I look for to determine the quality of the assessments my child experiences? Why is it important to see a variety of assessment methods used in my child's classroom? What does student involvement in assessment look like? What are productive ways to become involved in homework assignments? Chapter 4 describes the variety of classroom assessment methods and why each is used. We also look at productive and counterproductive homework practices.

What is a *standardized* test? Which of these tests do our children take in school, and what do they measure? How is standardized test information used? How do standardized tests and classroom assessments fit together? Measuring students' educational progress has never been easy and is becoming more challenging. Because the American public uses test results to develop opinions about the quality of schools, it is important to know that the assessments being used to form those opinions are accurate, and it is just as important to know what other indicators exist to help judge school quality. In Chapter 5 we explain the kinds of standardized tests students take and advocate for informed, careful use of test results.

How should the teacher/school/district communicate with us about our children's progress as learners? What factors should and should not be included in calculating report card grades? In what ways beyond test scores and grades can we learn about our children's progress? What role can students play in communicating about their own learning? Chapter 6 outlines answers to these questions.

Finally, in Chapter 7 we'll review key points from each chapter and link them to actions you can consider taking to help your children learn and to support assessment systems at the local level that promote student learning.

Throughout the book, we describe what a healthy, balanced assessment environment looks like in schools and classrooms. We offer ideas for how you as parents, educators, and community members can find out if this type of environment is in place in your schools. In this way, we hope to help you work with your child's teacher, school, district, and other parents and community members to get the best education possible for your children and *all* children in your community.

Chapter 1

Assessment in School Today

What Is Assessment and Why Is It Changing?

E veryone needs information to plan. Doctors need information about patients to plan treatments. Investors need information to help you invest your money. And educators need information about students' achievement to help them learn. *Assessment* is the process of collecting information. In our schools, it is the process of collecting evidence of student learning. That evidence may focus on individuals or groups of students, and it may come from one or more sources. Tests are the best-known tools for collecting that information. But tests are only one tool. Student oral presentations, projects, student interviews, writing samples, performance assessments, teacher observation, portfolios, and student self-assessment can all serve to collect accurate information about student learning.

Much about assessment in schools remains the same as it has always been: students study for tests, teachers calculate grades, and some students fare better than others. But much about assessment in schools is changing, too, in response to major shifts in thinking about education.

What we want schools to do is changing. The school's mission used to be one of sorting students from the highest to the lowest achiever. This allowed schools to serve the social function of easing citizens into the various segments of our social and economic system. The student's goal was to finish as high in the rank order as possible. Today, high schools still use grade-point averages to rank  students, but now we also ask schools to ensure the achievement of the largest possible number of students. Students are no longer just compared to each other to rank order them. Schools have now defined specific things students should know and be able to do. Assessment measures their ability to do those things. Each student's challenge is to meet these academic expectations, and the schools are to help every student do just that. It is this change in thinking about the mission of schools that underpins President Bush's mandate to "leave no child behind."

What we want students to know and be able to do is changing. What used to be the "basics" are no longer enough to function as a successful adult in our society. Participation in our nation's workforce requires a more complex web of basic skills, as well as skills beyond the basics. State and district learning goals increasingly reflect both knowledge and competencies needed to be successful in life beyond school. As a result, the assessment tools we use must be able to measure knowledge of the basics and skillful application of them. Assessments of these learning goals must also connect to life beyond school and therefore have changed to reflect situations in which such learning would be demonstrated.

We know more about testing and assessment. Traditionally, standardized tests have lacked depth. They have been designed to sample from a broad range of everything a student could know about a subject, but, for the most part, these tests haven't been designed to go deeply into students' understanding of specific content areas they have studied. Many standardized tests are limited by the multiple-choice format to measuring students' content knowledge and some reasoning patterns. As a result, a number of states and districts have developed their own standardized tests to probe more deeply into the skillful application of knowledge.

We have more information about uses of classroom assessment that bring about higher achievement. Assessment practices that encourage and improve learning have been around as long as education has been, but the education community has only recently had access to large numbers of studies that document their effectiveness. How many of us remember assessment from our school years as a joyful, exciting, productive, satisfying experience? It is likely that we remember multiple-choice questions, fill-in-the-blanks items, quizzes, and end of term exams that determine a final grade. We probably also recall feeling tense, anxious, or even fearful at times. Current research indicates that assessment doesn't have to be this way; it can be exciting, productive, and satisfying for teachers and students.

In understanding how assessment can function this other way, one of the challenges we face is our own past experiences being assessed in school, which may not have included assessment *for* learning. In the classroom, this kind of assessment seeks to inform students about themselves and their own learning, showing them exactly where they are in relation to the learning targets their teachers have set, and with the help of their teachers, knowing which steps to take next. Tests have their place in the classroom, but if that is all the assessment that is going on, our teachers and children are missing a huge portion of the power of assessment.

All of these changes have combined to make assessment today different than what we as students experienced. They bring the potential for much more powerful learning environments than we experienced growing up. It is important to keep these changes in mind as we learn about current assessment practices and how to build positive assessment environments for our students.

What Is the Purpose of Assessment?

Even if you have no children in school today, it is easy to notice that whatever else is different, students take more tests these days. To understand why, we'll start by asking, *What is the purpose of assessment?*

Most misuses of assessments (and assessment dollars) arise from an incomplete or vague answer to this question. The purpose of all assessments can be stated in one sentence: *Assessments provide results to inform decisions.* The problems arise when we fail to think through clearly the following questions: *Who needs the information? What information do they need? What decisions will they make?* No assessment should be designed, selected, or given without the assessor first answering those questions. To understand why we have so many assessments, we need to explore the range of possible answers. Figure 1.1 shows the users of assessment information within a series of concentric circles, with those closest to the actual learning at the center.

Figure 1.1 Users of Assessment

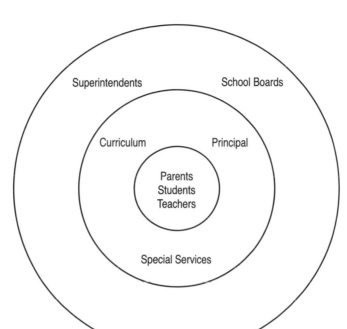

Who Needs Assessment Information?

Decision makers—Inner circle. Let's begin with those closest to the learning: parents and teachers. What kinds of decisions do they make? Parents use assessment information to decide what to do to support their child's learning, and teachers use it to assign report card grades. What other decisions do parents and teachers make on the basis of school assessment information? (Remember, assessment information can include test scores and grades, as well as written and oral comments from the teacher.) See how your thoughts compare to the decisions listed in Table 1.1.

Table 1.1 Sample Decisions Made on the Basis of School Assessment Information—Inner Circle

PARENTS	TEACHERS
Is my child learning new things?	Are my students improving?
Is my child succeeding?	What does this student need?
Is my child keeping up?	What student strengths can I build on?
Is my child doing enough at home to succeed in school?	How should I group my students?
Is there a change I need to recommend for my child?	Am I going too fast, too slowly, too far, not far enough?
Are we doing enough at home to support learning at school?	Am I improving as a teacher?
Does the teacher know what my child needs?	Did that teaching strategy work?
Is this teacher doing a good job?	What shall I say at parent–teacher conferences?
Is this a good school? A good district?	What report card grade do I assign?

Source: Adapted from *Student-Involved Classroom Assessment*, 3rd ed. (p. 32) by Richard J. Stiggins, 2001, Upper Saddle River, NJ: Merrill-Prentice Hall. Copyright © 2001 by Prentice-Hall, Inc. Adapted by permission.

What about students as decision makers? We almost never think of students as assessment users—most often we see them as the subjects of assessment. But what kinds of decisions do your children make based on assessment information?

Consider Andrea's experience with her long-term writing project in middle school. The teacher has graded it and handed it back, the words "garrulous and verbose" written at the top of the first page, along with many suggestions for improvement in the margins of the other pages. Andrea concludes she is not good at writing, and from now on, each time she has to write, it becomes harder. Andrea loves language, but hates writing.

How about Joe, who wants to be an architect? He takes Algebra II, but doesn't understand a number of the concepts taught and, even though he studies, performs poorly on test after test. He comes to believe that he is not good at math, and decides not to take any more math courses. When he realizes architecture requires more math, he concludes that he cannot become an architect.

Or Maria, a second-grade struggling reader. She receives accurate feedback about her progress, provided in a way that encourages her to keep learning. Her teacher tells her, "Here's what you are doing well and here's what we are going to work on next." Maria keeps at it because the assessment information she has received has led her to understand what good reading looks like and to see how she can get closer and closer to that goal.

Our children make crucial decisions daily, decisions that directly affect their own learning, based on assessment information coming from the teacher and the school. They decide whether they are succeeding, if they are improving over time, if they are capable of success, whether they like the subject, and whether they are going to continue learning. Their decisions are central to their learning. If they decide they are not capable of learning, if they decide to quit trying, no other decision maker, no matter the credentials, will be able to cause learning to happen. Students are the *most important decision makers* in the learning process (Table 1.2).

Decision makers—Middle circle. Less directly connected to the learning process, but still making decisions that affect the quality of schools are instructional leaders such as principals, curriculum directors, and special services directors. Table 1.3 samples some of the instructional support decisions they make. As you read through the list, notice how students' needs will not be met if our schools are unable to answer these questions.

Table 1.2 Sample Decisions Made on the Basis of School Assessment Information—The Heart of the Circle

STUDENTS
Am I succeeding?
Am I improving over time?
Do I understand what it means to succeed in this subject?
Am I good at this subject?
Do I like this subject?
What should I do next to succeed?
What help do I need?
Am I in control of my success?
Does my teacher think I'm capable of success?
Is the learning worth the effort?

Source: Adapted from *Student-Involved Classroom Assessment*, 3rd ed. (p. 32) by Richard J. Stiggins, 2001, Upper Saddle River, NJ: Merrill-Prentice Hall. Copyright © 2001 by Prentice-Hall, Inc. Adapted by permission.

Decision makers—Outer circle. Table 1.4 shows the policy makers who must have information about student learning as they make decisions to implement policies or laws and allocate resources. Notice that these decisions are also important to ensure that students' educational needs are met.

Decision makers—All circles. Taken together, all of these people use assessment information to make decisions that affect the learning of each student in our schools. Remove any one of them, or provide inaccurate or incomplete information, and learning will suffer.

Table 1.3 Sample Decisions Made on the Basis of School Assessment
Information—Middle Circle

PRINCIPAL	CURRICULUM DIRECTOR	SPECIAL SERVICES EDUCATORS
Is this teacher producing results in the form of student learning? How can I help this teacher improve? Is instruction in our building producing results? Are our students prepared for college and the workplace? How shall we allocate building resources to help students succeed?	Is our program of instruction working? What adjustments do we need to make in our curriculum?	Who qualifies for special educational services? Is our program of services helping students? What assistance does this student need to succeed?

Source: Adapted from *Student-Involved Classroom Assessment*, 3rd ed. (p. 33) by Richard J. Stiggins, 2001, Upper Saddle River, NJ. Merrill-Prentice Hall. Copyright © 2001 by Prentice-Hall, Inc. Adapted by permission.

Summative and Formative Decisions

These various decisions and decision makers need different
kinds of information delivered in different ways and at different
times to do their jobs. A helpful way to think about this collection of decisions is to conceive of them as serving either summative or formative purposes. *Summative* assessment reports
on the status of learning at a point in time. We think of these as
assessments *of* learning. *Formative* assessment, on the other
hand, serves the purpose of tracking and promoting learning
along the way—it is assessment *for* learning.

Table 1.4 Sample Decisions Made on the Basis of School Assessment Information—Outer Circle

SUPERINTEN-DENT	SCHOOL BOARD MEMBERS	STATE DEPTS OF EDUCATION	CITIZENS & LEGISLATORS
Are our programs of instruction producing results in terms of student learning? Is each building principal producing results? Which schools deserve or need more resources?	Are our students learning and succeeding? Is our superintendent producing results?	Are programs across the state producing results? Are individual school districts producing results?	Are our students achieving in ways that prepare them to become productive citizens?

Source: Adapted from *Student-Involved Classroom Assessment*, 3rd ed. (p. 33) by Richard J. Stiggins, 2001, Upper Saddle River, NJ: Merrill-Prentice Hall. Copyright © 2001 by Prentice-Hall, Inc. Adapted by permission.

Summative Assessment—Assessment of Learning

Summative assessment has as its main purpose to gather and report evidence of learning. It sums up the learning—it's a status report. It can take the form of a test at the end of a course given by a classroom teacher, a college admissions test, or a state- or district-mandated standardized test. All summarize student learning at the time of the assessment, and can help decision makers in certain ways. Much summative assessment is not intended to inform the classroom teacher about day-to-day instruction, or to help students become better learners. Rather, assessments *of* learning in the classroom most often are used to determine a grade. In some instances they are also

14

used to help determine placement into specific instructional groupings, such as special education or gifted and talented programs. Summative assessments *of* learning can take the form of tests, quizzes, projects, performances, interviews, reports, oral presentations; in short, any method of assessment can be used summatively. Results can be reported in a number of ways:

- A letter grade (A, B, C, etc.)

- A percent correct (78%)

- A percentile (65th %ile)

- A grade-point average (3.1)

- Another alphabet letter representing progress toward a standard (E, M, P, etc.)

- A number (1, 2, 3)

- A word representing a stage on a developmental continuum

These symbols function as a shorthand way to communicate about student learning, but they only work if we understand exactly what they mean. In Chapters 5 and 6 we give more detail about each of these ways to report on achievement.

We also rely on assessments *of* learning to inform accountability decisions. They tell us how much students have learned, whether standards are being met, and if educators have done the job they were hired to do. Assessments *of* learning dominate resource allocation in testing and assessment. We conduct them routinely at local, state, national, and international levels. Over the last 50 years in the United States alone, we have invested billions of dollars to deliver these tests and to ensure the accuracy of the scores. Even so, controversy surrounding these tests exists among community members, parents, and educators, which we will address later in this chapter.

Formative Assessment—Assessment for Learning

Assessment *for* learning occurs during teaching and learning as opposed to after it, and has ongoing improvement as its primary focus (Crooks 2001; Shepard 2001; Assessment Reform Group 1999). It uses day-to-day classroom assessment activities to involve students directly in their own learning, increasing their confidence and motivation to learn by emphasizing progress and achievement rather than failure and defeat (Stiggins 1999, 2001). Once students become involved, assessment *for* learning looks more like teaching than it does testing. It takes advantage of the power of assessment as an instructional tool that promotes learning rather than an event designed solely for the purpose of evaluating and assigning grades (Davies 2000). Teachers use assessment information formatively when they do such things as identify which concepts or skills students need more work with to plan further instruction; investigate the effectiveness of their own teaching practices; and provide regular feedback to students on their strengths and areas for improvement. Students engage in assessment *for* learning when they use assessment information to learn how to judge the quality of their own work and set goals for their own improvement. As you read Tables 1.5 and 1.6, notice that both categories of assessment are essential, in different ways, to a healthy educational environment.

The model of formative assessment we describe involves more than just assessing students more often. It goes beyond providing teachers with assessment results to revise instruction. In assessment *for* learning, both teacher and student use classroom assessment information to modify teaching and learning activities (Assessment Reform Group 1999).

Table 1.5 Key Differences

	ASSESSMENT *of* LEARNING	ASSESSMENT *for* LEARNING
REASONS FOR ASSESSING	Document individual or group achievement or mastery of standards; measure achievement status at a point in time for purposes of reporting	Increase achievement; to help students meet more standards; support ongoing student growth
TO INFORM	Others about students	Students about themselves
FOCUS OF ASSESSMENT	Achievement standards for which schools, teachers, and students are held accountable	Specific achievement targets selected by teachers that enable students to build toward standards
DRIVING FORCE	Accountability	Improvement
PLACE IN TIME	Event after learning is supposed to have happened	Process during learning

Table 1.6 Differences in Assessment Context

	ASSESSMENT *of* LEARNING	ASSESSMENT *for* LEARNING
PRIMARY USERS	Policy makers, program planners, supervisors, teachers	Students and teachers in partnership (coach guiding learner)
TYPICAL USES	Certify competence or sort students according to achievement for public relations, gatekeeper decisions, grading, graduation, or advancement	Help students see the target and how to hit it; help teachers diagnose and respond to student needs; help parents see progress over time
PRIMARY MOTIVATOR	Threat of punishment, promise of rewards	Belief that success is within reach with continued effort
TEACHER'S ROLE	Follow test administration procedures to ensure accuracy and comparability of results; use results to help students meet standards; interpret results for parents; teachers also build assessments for report card grading	Transform standards into classroom targets; inform students of targets; build assessments; adjust instruction based on results; involve students in assessment
STUDENT'S ROLE	Study to meet standards, take the test, strive for the highest possible score, avoid failure	Strive to understand the target; act on classroom assessment results to be able to do better next time

18

Teachers use assessment information formatively when they

- Pretest before a unit of study and adjust instruction for individuals or for the entire group

- Identify which students need more help

- Revise instruction based on assessment results

- Reflect on the effectiveness of their own teaching practices

- Confer with students regarding their strengths and areas needing improvement

- Facilitate peer tutoring, matching students who demonstrate understanding with those who do not

Students use assessment information formatively when they

- Engage in self-assessment, accurately describing where they are in their learning and where they need to go next

- Watch themselves grow by monitoring their own progress

- Describe their learning and their growth to others

It isn't the method of assessment that tells us whether it is a formative or summative assessment. Many assessment methods—tests, quizzes, performance tasks, writing essays, and data gathered through observation of skills and products— can be used either way. How the results are used tells us if the assessment is formative or summative.

Although formative assessment in the classroom does not serve all of the decision makers or users of assessment data, we need to understand the central role it plays in promoting further learning. This form of assessment can motivate and guide students in their progress, and help teachers gain the knowledge of each individual student in their class so as to focus instruction in specific ways.

Different Decisions, Different Assessments

So, why do we need classroom, school, district, state, national, and even international assessments? As we have shown, students need information about their learning to help them feel in control so they will keep trying. Teachers need information to see how to help students learn. School and district personnel need information to make programmatic and placement decisions. Policy makers need large-scale standardized testing information to make accountability decisions. Also, as states develop their own curriculum standards, many have developed companion assessment systems.

Here's the key point: one level or type of assessment will not necessarily provide the right kind of information for all of the decision makers listed above. That is why schools use a variety of assessments. How many assessments are needed for all purposes? Are we conducting too many assessments for certain needs and not enough for others? We believe that it is a good idea to ask, "Why so many?" if you think your school system is overtesting students. As your district or school responds, listen for an explanation of the *purpose* of each assessment—*who* will use the information and *what decisions* they will make on its basis. Is this clearly defined? Also listen for an explanation of *what kinds of learning* are measured on each assessment.

Testing for Accountability

The question "Why so many?" has another facet to it—the spike in large-scale standardized testing for accountability purposes. Today, political support for school accountability continues to rise at local, state, and national levels, fostered by the belief that increased large-scale testing will force improvement in the quality of our schools. As we showed earlier, these tests provide the information policy makers and educators need regarding the achievement of students and schools in order to make programmatic, instructional, and accountability driven decisions. They also allow comparisons to be made among students and among schools. In addition, standardized tests often serve as a foundation for the complex systems of sanctions and rewards applied in many districts and states across the country.

There are divergent views about the effectiveness of educational accountability testing in improving schools as well as about appropriate uses of the tests themselves. The issue is not accountability. That schools should publicly report their performance is beyond question in our minds; schools should provide evidence of how much and how well students are learning. If schools are failing the students they serve, it is right to compel those schools to improve.

The issue is whether large-scale standardized tests will improve learning. Some have argued that testing in this context is counterproductive, that it may actually widen the gap between successful and struggling students, instead of closing it. Some studies show that large-scale standardized testing has little impact on improving student learning (Shepard 2000). It is also a concern to some who believe that the tests are unfair to students in schools that are not capable of marshalling the financial resources that may be required to make the necessary improve-

ments. In this book, we do not enter the debate as to whether these tests are the right tools for the task. We do, however, believe the following about them: they are not an educational panacea. Effective as some believe they may prove to be when used as the fulcrum of accountability, tests by themselves will not succeed as the catalyst for producing a nation of high-performing schools.

Throughout this book we advocate for a companion approach to school improvement that we think needs to be present with large-scale accountability testing: assessment *for* learning. Research and experience argue strongly in favor of a national movement to use assessment to foster, not just to measure and grade, the achievement of every student. And, of all of the different decision makers and consumers of assessment results, the *student* must be considered the primary user of assessment information. This thinking is not yet the norm in classrooms and schools, but we think it should be. If we are sincere about wanting students to assume a level of responsibility for their own learning, they need to have information on which to act: information they understand; information that is accurate, immediate, and delivered in a way that encourages them to keep learning. Students who are actively involved in the assessment process learn from that experience and achieve at higher levels. Classroom practice aligns with research findings when teachers adopt a set of practices that puts student needs first and calls for strong student involvement in every facet of classroom assessment.

Assessment Literacy in the Schools

Because all of these uses of assessment are so crucial for student well-being, it is absolutely essential that assessment results—whether generated in the classroom or via external examination—be accurate. Any assessments our children take must meet certain standards of quality. Their developers must understand and apply those standards routinely. In other words, they must be *assessment literate*. Teachers and administrators who are assessment literate understand the difference between sound and unsound assessment, evaluation, and communication practices:

- They understand what assessment methods to use to gather dependable information about student achievement.

- They communicate assessment results effectively, whether using report card grades, test scores, portfolios, or conferences.

- They understand how to use assessment to maximize student motivation and learning by involving students as full partners in assessment, record keeping, and communication.

You may be surprised to learn that in a great many instances, neither teachers nor administrators have been trained to assess student achievement accurately, nor are they trained to interpret or use assessment results to maximize learning. Many have not been given the opportunity to learn, and therefore do not understand, the difference between sound and unsound assessment, evaluation, or grading practices. Neither are they aware of the principles of formative assessment, or assessment *for* learning. The research we'll describe in more detail in the next chapter finds that these assessment practices, the key to raising student achievement, are largely absent in classrooms.

And so, while we as parents and community members assume that teachers and schools know what, when, and how to assess fairly and accurately, this is often not the case. Many teachers are aware of this and welcome the opportunity to learn more. The growing frequency and concurrent demands of accountability-oriented state or local testing programs have resulted in local educators needing more than ever the knowledge and skill to use and to communicate evidence of learning in productive ways. They also need to understand options in preparing their students for these tests other than superficial test-prep programs or outdated versions of state tests.

Teachers are caught in a situation that deserves our help and understanding. The dilemma they face is how to raise scores on state tests without sacrificing real learning in the classroom. It needs to be made clear to all who have a stake in improving education the critical role that classroom assessment, assessment *for* learning, can play in improving student performance on the standardized assessments *of* learning. And even though the best teachers and principals may work to balance both demands, without having a solid background in assessment literacy it is not likely they will succeed.

Clearly this is a situation we must address if we are to avoid the real harm that can result from the inappropriate uses of standardized tests. It is a situation we must address if we are to realize the improved learning that can happen in every classroom where an assessment literate teacher applies the principles of assessment *for* learning.

Chapter 1 — Important Ideas

- *Assessment* is the process of gathering evidence of student achievement.

- A variety of people need assessment information in schools today—at the classroom, school, and policy levels.

- The role of assessment in school improvement continues to grow toward greater reliance on standardized assessments *of* learning. However, assessments *for* learning offer greater promise of helping students succeed.

- Schools today are being held accountable for helping students meet standards, not merely sorting students into a rank order.

- All assessments need to provide accurate information about student achievement if they are to serve users well. For that to happen, all educators need to be assessment literate, understanding the principles of sound classroom assessment practice.

- We have used the majority of our assessment resources to fund standardized testing at the local, state, and national levels. The accuracy and power of classroom assessments, and consequently student learning, have suffered as a result.

Chapter 2

Connecting Student Motivation and Assessment

How Does Motivation Work?

How do you motivate kids to do things? Imagine you are trying to get your children to clean up their bedrooms. Some clean up their rooms because it's a habit, because it's the right thing to do, or because they like a tidy room. Some do it because their allowance or a privilege is dependent on a clean room. Others do it to avoid a negative consequence. And then there are those who will wait us out, hoping that we will get tired of asking, telling, pleading and finally go in and do it ourselves.

The motivational forces at work behind the scenes can be categorized as either intrinsic (internal) or extrinsic (external). When we are relying on *intrinsic* motivation to get something done, our children *want to* do the activity, either because they value the outcome (a clean room, for example), or because they enjoy the act of doing it (putting things away, finding long-lost treasures). If our children are not intrinsically motivated to accomplish the task, we rely on *extrinsic* motivation. In this case, our children *will* do the activity, either to get the reward they have earned (allowance, privilege), or to avoid the consequence of not doing it (no television, no Internet). And when neither intrinsic nor extrinsic motivation works, the task does not get done unless we do it for them.

Assessment as a Motivator in School

What strategies do schools use to motivate children to learn, and how well do they work? One traditional approach is to use grades as extrinsic motivators. Let's follow the line of thought when grades function as rewards: "If you work hard (desired behavior), you will learn well (desired outcome), and if you learn well, you will get good grades (reward). Get good grades and you will graduate (reward). Graduate with good grades and you will get into college/get a good job (reward)." This system of rewards appears to work well for some students. Those who generally get good grades will continue to work for good grades.

Let's follow the line of thought when grades function as punishments: "If you don't work hard (undesired behavior), you will not do well (undesired outcome), and if you don't do well, you will get low grades (punishment). If you get low grades, you won't graduate (punishment). If you don't graduate, you won't get into college/get a good job (punishment)." The goal is that students will work harder to avoid the punishment in the future, and this does happen in some cases. Some students do study harder and try to do better the next time, but others don't. Low grades no longer work as a deterrent for those who have repeatedly experienced them. The motivational effects of grades are unpredictable, at best, and are not likely to work in the direction we hope for.

This same line of thought also underlies uses of large-scale standardized testing for accountability purposes. We may hope that low performance will spur greater effort, which will result in higher levels of achievement. This appears not to be the case for large numbers of low-performing students, however. What might you predict will happen when students score low year after year on publicly reported standardized tests? What happens to their motivation to learn and belief in their ability to learn? Are those students likely to want to keep trying? Are they likely to work harder to ensure that it doesn't happen again?

The test-taking anxiety that accompanies "raise the bar" testing for public accountability—anxiety that is intended to motivate students to do well—does not always lead to maximum effort or learning for students (Stiggins 2001). "When the going gets tough, the tough get going" is a maxim we are all familiar with, and it is true for some students. Increased pressure works as a motivator for those students whose academic history leads them to expect success if they try harder. What happens to those who struggle as learners? For students whose academic histories include a great deal of public failure, the result of raise the bar testing is a growing sense of futility. When faced with expectations even greater than the ones that they were failing at before, they regard the test as another episode of public embarrassment to be endured. Repeated experiences of failure cause many students to adopt an "I don't care" attitude to protect themselves, and the punishment has lost its power to motivate desired behavior. Implementing higher standards is a good thing; expecting the intimidation of accountability testing to cause students to reach those standards is not.

Clearly there are instances when assessment can destroy the motivation of some students. Indeed, assessment can be the fastest, most effective way to destroy motivation, but it can also be used as a tool to bring motivation back, even when it has been destroyed in the past. To stop the harm and promote the good, we first have to recognize that all students don't respond in the same way to the use of grades or test scores as threats of punishment or promises of reward. Then we need to see how assessment can be used differently. To do that, we'll explore what the educational research community knows about how to create productive links among assessment, motivation, and student achievement, and how to avoid the destructive links.

Research on Assessment, Motivation, and Student Achievement

In 1998, two British researchers, Paul Black and Dylan Wiliam, completed a comprehensive review of over 250 international studies exploring the connection between formative assessment practices and increased achievement. Three questions guided their inquiry: (1) Does improved formative assessment cause better learning? (2) Do formative assessment practices need improving? (3) Is there evidence about how to improve formative assessment?

Does Improved Formative Assessment Cause Better Learning?

Their findings read like the proverbial good news–bad news story. The good news first: Improved formative assessment can raise achievement significantly for students at all levels. (In these studies, increases in levels of achievement were measured by standardized tests.) The achievement gains of students experiencing formative assessment are much larger than gains from other well-known interventions, such as reducing class size. Students at all achievement levels learn significantly more when their teachers use good formative assessment. The greatest and most positive effects are found for the lowest achievers, clearly giving schools facing gaps in achievement between low-socio-economic and other students concrete action they can take to address the problem. Another piece of good news: these learning gains will show up on standardized tests.

Do Formative Assessment Practices Need Improving?

Less positive news comes with the answer to the second question. The studies show that most teachers simply do not know how to practice high-quality formative assessment. Black and Wiliam report that much of the assessment in classrooms today still encourages learning at a low basic level, and that quantity of student work is often more important than quality of work to teachers. The majority of teachers' classroom assessments are summative—they model the design of external tests, or assessments *of* learning. Further, most classroom assessments give greater attention to grading than to providing students with useful advice for improvement.

Is There Evidence About How to Improve Formative Assessment?

With that somewhat dim report, the answer to the third question begins to brighten the picture again. Black and Wiliam suggest three courses of action for improving classroom assessment practice:

- Improve the quality and accuracy of the assessments themselves.

- Change how feedback is given to students—increase descriptive feedback and decrease evaluative feedback.

- Involve students in classroom assessment.

Accurate Classroom Assessments

Teachers need to know how to choose and develop assessments that give an accurate picture of student achievement. How well does Sam write? Has Kelsey learned the specific math skills desired? This is called *assessment literacy*. As you will remember from Chapter 1, we define assessment literacy as the ability to provide accurate information about a student's learning, in ways that encourage the learner to keep learning. Black and Wiliam's (1998) findings show that educators need the opportunity to learn how to write or select good assessments, and then how to use assessments as teaching tools. We discuss ensuring assessment accuracy in Chapter 4.

Descriptive Feedback

Think about the kinds of feedback students often get about their learning: a letter grade, a percentage, a check, a smiley face, the words "good job" or "needs work." Many times there is no accompanying explanation of what features of the work earned the evaluation. This is what Black and Wiliam (1998) refer to as *evaluative feedback*. It can have a valid use in learning—to sum up learning over time, but it does not function as a tool to increase learning. In some cases, evaluative feedback reduces motivation and inhibits further achievement.

The researchers found, however, that *descriptive feedback*—specific comments about the quality or characteristics of the work itself—has a positive impact on motivation and learning. Descriptive feedback can point out strengths or weaknesses. It offers specific information to students about the quality of the work they have done, helping them understand what they are doing right and what they can do to improve. Descriptive feedback on a writing assignment might look like this: "Your use of vivid details when you explained the frog race made it seem real"; "The sentence structure of this paper gives it a sense of rhythm and flow"; or, "You have allowed run-on sentences to creep into your writing."

To understand the different effects evaluative and descriptive feedback can have on a child, think about a fourth-grade child who gets back a math paper with a " –7" and an "N" (for Needs work) at the top. When asked what this means, she says, "I'm not good at math." Looking more closely at the paper, you notice that several problems test her ability to subtract numbers requiring "borrowing," several problems relate to geometric shapes, several problems test place value, several problems ask that she write fractions for the shaded part of a shape, and several problems require her to represent pictures by writing number sentences. Instead of the " –7" and "N," what if the feedback on the paper were broken down, so that she could see exactly what she is good at and what she needs to work on?

Descriptive feedback might look like this: "Things you did well: recognized geometric shapes, understood place value, wrote accurate number sentences. Things to work on: writing fractions and subtracting with borrowing."

Which of these two forms of feedback would be more helpful to your own child? Which would you prefer to receive? Both strong and struggling math students need to be able to say what they know, and both need to know what to work on next. That's what feedback ought to do for the learner—let her know, in specific terms, what she has learned and what she needs to focus on. Which of these two forms of feedback would be more likely to *motivate* your child to keep learning math?

What about comments such as, "Great effort!" or "You tried hard!"? They are a form of evaluative feedback, often intended to motivate students who are not achieving, even though they are trying. Although well-intentioned, this type of feedback does not work to enhance learning, for two reasons. First, rewarding effort without achievement sends the message that trying hard, rather than learning, is what matters. The result? Students who strive to look like they're working hard. Second, research studies have shown that feedback such as this, focused on the *learner*, rather than on the *learning*, can have a negative effect on motivation to learn. When students who perform poorly on a task hear only "Great effort!," they tend to conclude they are not capable of succeeding. They tried, it didn't work, and the only information from the assessor is that they tried. Providing this kind of feedback can be more detrimental to future learning than providing none (Atkin, Black, & Coffey 2001).

When the goal is to maximize student motivation and learning, productive feedback

- Tells students where they are right, identifying strengths and providing information that helps students develop them further

- Describes why an answer is correct or incorrect in terms students understand

- Tells students where they are now relative to the defined learning goals

- Explains in clear, constructive language what students need to do to improve

- Helps students generate their own strategies for improvement

It is neither the presence nor amount of feedback that increases learning; it is the direct connection to achievement targets that makes the difference (Atkin, Black, & Coffey 2001). Descriptive feedback guides students toward the achievement targets, helps them stay in touch with how close they are, and identifies adjustments they should make to hit those targets.

Student Involvement in Assessment

The third of Black and Wiliam's (1998) findings, that increasing student involvement in the assessment process will result in increased learning, is an unfamiliar concept to most of us. Doesn't it seem like cheating at first glance? Let us be quick to say what student involvement in assessment is *not*: It is *not* students controlling decisions about what will be learned. It is *not* students controlling what will be tested, and it is *not* students controlling decisions about what their grades will be.

Imagine you are in a boat, rowing a group of children across a lake, one child at a time. The first child you take wants to do all the rowing. Your job is to provide guidance about the boat's progress toward the destination—"You're headed right for the landing spot," and suggestions for when the boat strays off course—"Pull a little harder on the left oar." The second child wants to row alongside you. You each take an oar, and you adjust your rowing to that of the child so you can steer a straight course, while coaching periodically—"Good job of pulling evenly," or "Dip the oar in a little deeper as you row." The third child sits quietly in the boat and allows you to row without disturbance. The fourth child bounces around and drags body parts through the water, making rowing a chore. The fifth child won't stay in the boat, so the only way you can reach the destination is to tie this child (who is of course wearing a life preserver) to the stern and row with all your might.

Wouldn't it be great if all students felt about school the way the first child felt about rowing the boat? She needs only to see the target and she's off. The second child needs to see the target and benefits from descriptive feedback on his rowing. The third child needs to see the target, understand that part of her job is to row, and develop the confidence to take up one of the oars. The fourth and fifth children have disengaged entirely. Research studies have shown us that formative assessment practices, especially student involvement in assessment, can help all children, but the results are most dramatic with "rowboat children four and five," the struggling or disengaged learners.

So what *is* student involvement in assessment? The practices we know to be most powerful focus on students as users of assessment information and teacher feedback to be in control of their own progress and learning. Central to these practices is a set of three questions every learner asks and answers regularly: Where am I trying to go? Where am I now relative to that target? What specific action do I need to take to close the gap? (Sadler 1989; Atkin, Black, & Coffey 2001).

Where Am I Trying to Go?

Learning is easier when students understand what it is they are trying to achieve, the purpose of achieving it, and what success looks like. Therefore, the first step in meaningful student involvement is to let students know where we are headed with them. The child sitting in the rowboat, content to let you row, may have no inkling of the destination, and no concept that he should even know the destination. "Aren't I just supposed to sit here? You do the thinking, teacher, and I'll do whatever you say." We believe, in the words of Rick Stiggins, that "students can hit any target they can see and that holds still for them." Schools must communicate the learning goals to students in understandable language, both in advance of teaching and as lessons unfold. (We describe the learning goals schools hold for students in depth in Chapter 3.)

Where Am I Now Relative to That Target?

Students can use teacher feedback from formative assessments to understand where they are relative to the defined learning targets. It is crucial that "course correction" feedback be planned to encourage learners to keep going—it should both describe what learners are doing well and offer pointers for improvement.

Additionally, students can practice comparing their work to high-quality models, identifying the differences. Further, they can participate in classroom discussions that review what has already been taught, or respond to questions asking them to reflect individually on what they have learned relative to the targets. All of these strategies help students learn to ascertain where they are and where they need to be, an awareness central both to their motivation to learn and to their ultimate success.

What Specific Action Do I Need to Take to Close the Gap?

Assessment *for* learning helps students know what to do to move from their current position to the final learning goal (Clark 2001). For students to meet learning goals it is essential to have their full participation in analyzing the assessment data, understanding the target, and planning the action to achieve the next goal. Students must use questioning strategies to close the gap between where they are and where they need to be:

- What do I need to change in my work to improve its quality?

- What specific help do I need to make these changes?

- From whom can I get help?

- What resources do I need?

A steady flow of descriptive feedback to students permits continuous self-assessing around what constitutes quality. Keeping students connected to a vision of quality as the unit of study progresses helps them formulate their next steps in learning (Sadler 1989).

Self-assessment and reflective thinking are within the grasp and capabilities of almost every student. Few of us were exposed to this kind of assessment environment in our youth. More often than not our experiences reflect an assessment environment that had at its core a view of teaching and learning that doesn't work for the majority of students today: the teacher teaches and then tests. To maximize the learning, maximize the anxiety. If students don't learn at the preestablished pace, too bad. The teacher and class move on; students who don't learn simply finish low in the rank order. Today, assessment *for* learning encourages teachers to teach, to assess progress along the way, and to adjust instruction to benefit *all* students (Shepard 2001).

Assessment can engender fear, anxiety, and feelings of failure. But it need not be so. In the hands of trained teachers it can instead be a set of daily experiences that breeds confidence, reveals to the learner the patterns and characteristics of her own learning, and deeply involves the learner in assessment itself, monitoring and communicating to others her own progress along the way.

How can we as parents know if student-involved assessment practices are in place in our schools? If they are, it's likely the daily routine includes one or more of the following activities:

* Teachers working directly with students to determine the attributes of good performance

- Students using criteria and rubrics to evaluate the quality of anonymous work, and then to identify strengths and weaknesses in their own work

- Teachers using diagnostic assessments at the beginning of learning

- Teachers involving students in creating practice tests

- Students drafting practice test "blueprints" based on their understanding of the learning targets they are to hit and the essential concepts in material to be learned

- Students accumulating evidence of their own improvement in growth portfolios

- Students talking about their growth and knowing when they are getting close to success

- Students involved in parent–teacher conferences

- Students realizing their own next steps for learning

This only works if teachers clearly know the targets students are to hit, have accurate information about student achievement, know how to provide descriptive feedback, and know how to help students self-assess well. All of these things can be taught to practicing teachers and students in teacher preparation programs. It is an issue that must be addressed by policy makers if assessment systems that balance assessment *of* and assessment *for* learning are to become a reality.

Chapter 2 — Important Ideas

- Not all students respond to the intimidation of high-stakes testing with greater effort.

- Assessment environments that balance assessment *of* and *for* learning work best to maintain student success, confidence, and effort.

- Assessment *for* learning environments rely on student-involved assessment, record keeping, and communication to keep students on track and trying.

- Assessment *for* learning relies on descriptive, rather than judgmental, feedback to help students see how to succeed.

- Because of a lack of opportunity to learn the principles of effective classroom assessment, many teachers do not know how to implement formative assessment practices.

Chapter 3

What Students Learn: Standards, Curriculum, and Learning Targets

We expect a lot from our schools and teachers in every area of their performance. And when it comes to the curriculum, the written guides that specify what it is that teachers teach and students should learn, our expectations may be at their highest. Beyond the basic math, science, social studies, reading, and writing knowledge and skills that are uniformly valued for every classroom, there are many competing interests from inside and outside the schoolhouse for instructional time. World languages, moral decency, music and the arts, citizenship, sexuality education, character education, substance abuse prevention, service learning, study skills, technology, and many other topics vie for attention. Even without organizational and external pressures, most teachers feel a measure of internal tension to "cover" everything they personally deem important. And, on top of this, teachers struggle to balance "deep understanding" with mastery of the "necessary factual knowledge." "So much to teach, so little time" is a frustrating truism for many teachers.

As parents, community members, and educators, we may disagree on exactly what is most important for teachers to teach and students to learn. But even with the diverse opinions regarding what is important, we may agree on one thing: Given the current structure of our educational system (the number of school days per year, the number of hours in the school day, average class size, etc.), we can't fit everything that we value into a K–12 experience.

Therefore, with classroom instructional time being at a premium, it is absolutely essential that districts and schools clearly define in every subject what students will be expected to learn. Without written curricula to act as the roadmap for teaching and learning, the risk increases that students will have vastly different learning experiences from teacher to teacher and grade to grade. The lack of coherence builds into a greater and greater problem each year students experience it. Lack of a clear curriculum alone is responsible for a portion of the achievement gap among students. This lack produces high school graduates with widely different sets of knowledge, skills, and levels of preparation for further education and the job market. In the absence of a written curriculum, the precious and limited time that is available to learn can be wasted and cannot be recovered.

Our schools should be held accountable for more than just their test scores. In our drive for students to attain higher standards, we need to make sure our local school community has thoughtfully answered the question, "Higher standards for what learning?"

What Is a Curriculum?

This chapter will help you understand the curriculum, or learning expectations, in your schools and what makes it so important. Schools use many different names to label what our students are to learn. Depending on the locale, the terms can be interchangeable or differently used. For the purposes of this book we'll use the following terms in the following ways:

Content Standards

These are broad statements in each subject area (mathematics, English, reading, social studies, science, health, art, music, physical education, etc.) identifying what students should know and be able to do. They are most often developed by states and/or school districts. In addition, content standards are written by national organizations such as the National Council of Teachers of Mathematics (NCTM). An example of a content standard in mathematics is, *Understands and applies basic and advanced properties of the concept of measurement.*

Curriculum

The *curriculum* is a more specific version of the content standards, usually designed for each subject area at an individual grade level. A curriculum is made up of statements of the objectives, or learning goals, to be taught in that subject. The previous math content standard might be supported by a grade two curriculum objective such as, *Understands the basic measures: length, width, height, weight, and temperature.*

Learning Targets

These are the most specific forms of learning expectations that define the objectives of daily lessons. They are the smaller, teachable and assessable parts of learning that make up the larger whole of curriculum objectives. Learning targets for individual lessons underpin and support the content standards, leading students up to the place where they are ready to demonstrate that they can meet the standards. A second-grade learning target that would contribute to accomplishment of the math content standard and curriculum objective examples would be, *Measures length to the nearest inch and centimeter.*

What's Different About Curriculum Today?

In the previous chapter we explored why assessment has changed over the last decade. One of the major reasons we noted is that the curriculum itself has changed; at state and local levels it now includes learning expectations that are not so easily assessed. Table 3.1 captures some of the fundamental shifts in curriculum that in turn have affected assessment.

These shifts have resulted in a need and a desire to measure, not just what students *know*, but what they *can do* with what they know. We ask them to know certain things and we want them to apply that knowledge in ways that reflect the changing demands of the twenty-first century workplace and an increasingly diverse society. We still want students to know facts. However, content standards today also call for students to use that knowledge to form deeper understandings, to compare and contrast, to analyze, and to evaluate. Other standards call for them to use knowledge to perform skillfully and to create products that are of high quality. Consequently, our schools must be able to assess the content knowledge as well as the

Table 3.1 Shifts in Curriculum

FROM	TO
• Unclear or unpublished expectations	• Uniform standards published for all to see
• Student left to guess at keys to success	• Students are taught keys to success
• Little connection to life beyond school	• Lays foundation for lifelong learning
• Defines material to be covered	• Defines material to be learned
• Much variation in curriculum expectations across teachers	• Consistent expectations across teachers
• Emphasis on content details	• Emphasis on depth of mastery
• Emphasis on memorization	• Emphasis on understanding
• Little awareness of connection to previous or future grade levels	• Continuous progress across grade levels
• Designed with belief that students learn passively	• Designed to acknowledge that learning requires active involvement

complex thinking and problem solving, performance skills, and product development capabilities that make up today's academic standards (Stiggins 2001).

Classroom Learning Targets: Four Categories

Because the increasingly broader range of learning targets presents a greater assessment challenge for schools, let's give these learning targets a closer look. We divide them into four categories—knowledge, reasoning, skill, and product—to help you understand the differences among *kinds* of learning expectations in place today.

Knowledge Targets

Knowledge learning targets represent the basic subject matter knowledge that provides the foundation for each subject: mathematics, social studies, science, literature, health, and so on. Examples include knowing multiplication facts, the three branches of government, the parts of an insect, and the spelling of commonly used words. Knowledge targets can be more complex than these, including targets that call for understanding concepts, such as when to use a Venn diagram in a math problem solution, the system of checks and balances in our government, the workings of a food web, and being able to identify the main characters in a story. At their heart, they are about recalling information from memory that is important to the practice of one or more subjects.

We have a second kind of knowledge learning target because, although some information must be memorized—be learned outright—it is more practical to know how to *find* other kinds of information. Our children also must learn to access sources outside their own memory. Increasingly in our era, we cannot store everything we need to know in our memory banks. A great deal of important knowledge we simply look up, and it is sufficient that we know where to find it. Knowing how to find information is a second way of knowing, and appears as knowledge targets requiring students to learn how to find information using reference materials, the Internet, and other sources.

Reasoning Targets

Beyond knowing something, knowing where to find it, and understanding it, we want our children to use their knowledge to *reason and solve practical problems*. Each content area in school has patterns of reasoning central to the practice of that subject in life beyond school. For example, think beyond the facts we learned in social studies class; think about what social studiers *do*. What do people who major in one of the social studies subjects do for a living? Political scientists, sociologists, economists, historians, pollsters, lawyers, geographers— what kinds of reasoning are required to succeed in these fields? Historians, for example, must be able to compare different accounts of an event, evaluate the credibility of each source, and draw a conclusion about what is most likely to have happened. Therefore, a social studies curriculum will include reasoning learning targets such as *compare*, *evaluate*, and *draw conclusions*. Reasoning targets build on the knowledge base: there is no such thing as "knowledge-free" reasoning. Our children's curriculum in each subject should represent both the important knowledge from that subject and also the kinds of reasoning necessary to the application of the subject in life beyond school.

Skill Targets

In the majority of school subjects, a third kind of target, *skill* targets, forms a part of important learning. In reading, students must learn how to read certain words by sight (knowledge), how to generalize from specific instances to a broader context (reasoning), and also how to read aloud with expression (a skill). In physical education class, students may learn the rules of volleyball (knowledge) as well as how to serve the ball (a skill). In a Japanese language class, students memorize certain words and learn about correct word order (knowledge), and also may learn how to converse with a shopkeeper in a store (a skill). In a biology class, students may learn about classifications of plants (knowledge), how to compare different plants (reasoning), and how to create a slide for use under a microscope (a skill). Skill learning targets build on and require a base of knowledge and reasoning.

Product Targets

In addition, most school subjects include *product* learning targets, wherein we ask students to use their knowledge and reasoning abilities to create quality products. Examples of product learning targets include writing a research report in English class, writing an hypothesis to guide an experiment in science class, creating a graph to represent data in mathematics class, and creating a museum-type display to explain a historical event in social studies class. In each case, the product itself is important to the practice of the subject in life beyond school. As with skill targets, product targets build on knowledge and reasoning targets. They often build on skill targets, as well.

These four kinds of learning targets represent the range of achievement expectations our children will encounter over the course of their education (Table 3.2).

Table 3.2 Sample Achievement Expectations

ACHIEVEMENT TARGET	KNOW AND UNDERSTAND	REASON	SKILLS	PRODUCTS
READING	Sight vocabulary; background knowledge required by text	Process the text and comprehend meaning	Oral reading fluency	
WRITING	Vocabulary needed to communicate; Mechanics of usage; Knowledge of topic	Choose words and syntactic elements to convey message; Evaluate text quality	Letter formation; Keyboarding skills	Samples of original text
MUSIC	Instrument mechanics; Musical notation	Evaluate tonal quality	Instrument fingering; Breath control	Original composition written in musical notation
SCIENCE	Science facts and concepts	Hypotheses testing; Classifying species	Manipulate lab apparatus correctly	Written lab report; Science fair model
MATH	Number meaning; Math facts; Numeration systems	Identify and apply algorithms to solve problems	Use manipulatives while problem solving	Graph representing data

Source: Adapted from *Student-Involved Classroom Assessment*, 3rd ed. (p. 77) by Richard J. Stiggins, 2001, Upper Saddle River, NJ: Merrill-Prentice Hall. Copyright © 2001 by Prentice-Hall, Inc. Adapted by permission.

All of these learning targets together form not just the basis for a balanced curriculum, but the foundation for quality assessment that ensures students can use what they know in productive ways. Having clear learning targets is essential if teachers are to use assessment to chart a progression of learning paths for individuals and groups of students, to check progress and provide feedback along the way, to be alerted to obstacles individuals may face in their journey, and to recognize and celebrate when students have reached the destination. If the targets are unclear or missing, none of this is possible.

Dividing learning targets into four categories provides a helpful way to understand why teachers use different assessment methods. Selecting appropriate methods of assessment to measure each target can increase our knowledge of student achievement, allowing us to form a more complete and accurate picture of student learning. It's actually a requirement for assessment quality, and we'll explain it in the next chapter.

Who Benefits When Curriculum Is Defined?

Rachel's mom: "What did you do in school today?"

Rachel: "Well, we did reading."

Rachel's mom: "What did you learn in reading?"

Rachel: "I don't know. We read."

Brad's mom: "What did you do in school today?"

Brad: "Well, we did reading."

Brad's mom: "What did you learn in reading?"

Brad: "We learned how to compare two characters in a story."

Rachel and Brad are in two different classrooms in the same school, learning how to read. They both participated in the same reading activities today. Yet Brad knows what the intended learning was and Rachel does not, because Brad's teacher has distinguished between an activity (reading) and the actual learning target (comparing two characters), and has also communicated the learning target to her students.

Benefits to Teaching

Rachel's experience illustrates an age-old problem that has been, in part, the result of poorly written curriculum or no curriculum at all: teaching to an activity instead of teaching to a predefined set of learning targets. Students often answer the "What-did-you-do-in-school-today" question with a list of topics: "whales," "Native Americans," "Africa," or "fractions." They are not able to say what specifically *about* whales was the intended learning. Is the topic of whales used as the vehicle to teach an understanding of animal habitats, compare-and-contrast reasoning, report writing? Was the topic chosen because it was well suited to the intended learning targets? Or did the teacher select "whales" because it's the children's favorite topic, one that he has a background in, or one with plenty of fun activities for students to do? We do want the topics our children study to be of high interest, taught by those prepared to teach them, with interesting activities incorporated wherever possible. Those are all good reasons to choose a topic of study. But they do not define the learning: "whales" is not a learning target.

Without a well-written, clearly defined set of learning targets in place grade by grade, our schools' teachers may be teaching topics—miscellaneous collections of facts about a series of subcategories of knowledge in each subject. When it comes time to assess the learning, assessment becomes a scramble to grade whatever students produced in response to the activities, but there can be no reliable statement of what each student learned, because the activities were not designed or selected with learning targets in mind.

At this point, you may be thinking, "Isn't that what textbooks are supposed to take care of? Don't they lay out important things to be learned chapter by chapter, unit by unit? And don't they come with tests that match the content?" Our answers are

"No, yes, and yes." It is true that textbooks are designed around a collection of learning targets, and often they come with ready-made assessments to measure achievement of those learning targets. It is *not* true that textbooks can stand in for a curriculum, for a number of reasons.

First and most importantly, the content of most textbooks on the market today has been carefully selected to represent anything and everything a school district or state conceivably could want taught about the subject at a grade level. In selecting a textbook series for adoption, a district or state looks for the best match to its content standards. Not every district or state has the same content standards for each grade level in each subject, so textbook developers look to include as much as possible. Therefore, in many cases, the content of the textbook represents much more than can be taught and learned in one year.

When teachers are given the assignment of completing the text by the end of the year, many feel forced to proceed at a pace that outstrips learning for some students. This alone can be the cause of some students being left behind—the teacher's need to cover all the material in the text. Or, if teachers decide to pace the teaching so that students have time to learn, they must select certain portions to teach and certain portions to leave out. Without a curriculum in place to guide the selection, we have no guarantee that what is most important will make the cut, and the course of study will not be consistent from class to class. In this situation, in a subject such as math, students going on to the next grade from different classes will come with very different knowledge bases, and your child may be less well prepared than another because of her previous teacher's individual curriculum decisions. The written curriculum works as a guide, enabling teachers to select wisely what they will teach from all that could be taught. And as important, it puts a frame around what teachers are supposed to assess.

Benefits to Learning

"What did you do in school today?"

"We did math." Or: "We did decimals." Or: "We did page 152." Or: "We learned how to read decimals and put them in order."

"Math" is a *subject*; "decimals" is a *topic*; "page 152 in the math book" is a *resource*; "read decimals and put them in order" is a *learning target*. Notice the differences?

We believe the strongest reason for having a written curriculum in place is so that students can know what they are expected to be learning, track their own progress, and set goals for their own further efforts. Without this knowledge, our children are unable to become the self-reliant learners we want them to be. And we as parents will not know how to support our young or not-so-young learners.

Consider Brianna's and Jevon's experiences learning how to spell. Brianna knows she's learning spelling, but Jevon knows he's learning how to spell words with the "long *a* sound." Both have done well with the "short *a* sound" words (*cat*), and both are having initial difficulty with the "long *a* sound" words (*late*). When asked to report on their progress as spellers, Brianna only knows she used to be good at spelling and now she's not. Jevon knows he's having trouble with "long *a* sound" words, but he is good at spelling "short *a* sound" words. Brianna may think she has to "try harder," or study more words. She will want to get better, but will not have enough information to direct her efforts. Jevon, on the other hand, will be able to focus his studying, and Jevon's parents will know what to help him with at home. He can tell them! Even though both students are experiencing the same learning "hump," Brianna is a discouraged learner in the making, while Jevon is developing confidence in himself as a learner.

Benefits to Testing for Accountability

When the test used for accountability purposes is an accurate reflection of the content standards established at the state level, then creating a local curriculum that aligns with the state content standards produces the following benefits:

- Students have the opportunity to learn those things their learning is judged by.

- Results from accountability tests will match results from classroom assessments.

- Test scores will rise.

Here's how. When classroom assessments match the district curriculum, when the district curriculum is aligned to the state content standards, and the large-scale summative assessments used for accountability purposes have been selected or designed to match those same content standards, our schools are testing and reporting progress on what they are teaching. Research repeatedly shows that, when teachers map out their instruction using a well-written curriculum, and then choose teaching materials and lessons that address the specific learning targets, student achievement increases. Teaching has a much greater influence on achievement than all socioeconomic factors combined. The biggest obstacle to achievement, including achievement as measured by accountability testing, is not whatever

background a student brings to school. Effective teaching can overcome even the most daunting achievement gaps, and it begins with a well-written curriculum (Schmoker 2002).

An aligned written, taught, and tested curriculum eliminates the weeks, or even months of frantic efforts to "prepare" students for the big state test coming up next month, because a portion of what they are learning as a part of regular classroom instruction will be tested on the standardized test. As a result, there are no surprises for students or parents on state tests results: those scores reflect the level and quality of performance students have already demonstrated in the classroom.

This only applies when the accountability test *has been created or selected to measure the specific content standards in place.* These tests are usually described as "criterion referenced," and we explain them in Chapter 5. (Adding "high stakes" to these tests may reduce or negate the benefits a well-written curriculum offers. We discuss this also in Chapter 5.) In addition, *the content standards and the local curriculum must actually measure important learning.* If the state standards lead to a local curriculum that is too broad to teach in the school year, if the curriculum is poorly written, so that teachers must puzzle over the intent of each phrase, or if the local curriculum is not aligned to state standards and assessments, students will not have had the opportunity to gain the learning identified as important to teach and measure.

How Parents Can Learn About the Written Curriculum

Most parents have probably experienced an Open House or a Curriculum Night or some similar back-to-school event where teachers describe what the year has in store for their students. You might read through course objectives for the year, look at the books your child will use, and even hear about how your child's learning will be assessed. Many schools schedule an event early in the fall to explain what children will be working on during the year. If you don't have the opportunity to learn about your child's achievement expectations through a school event, you can request a copy of the curriculum for your child's grade from your school or district office.

How the curriculum is written and organized in each school can vary greatly. We recommend you look for the following features. First, there *is* a written curriculum. A good written curriculum is very specific, representing knowledge, reasoning, skill, and product learning targets (where appropriate). It is aligned with state standards. There is a "translation" of the curriculum standards for parents—a document written in everyday language to communicate the grade-level learning expectations clearly. It is not just a restatement of the multiyear benchmarks from the state, a collection of goals, or general list of topics. Not all parents and community members may feel the need to know the details of the grade-level curriculum in their local schools. However, each of us should be concerned if that level of specificity is not available to those who need it and to those who are interested.

We parents can help our children more productively if we ask the following questions:

1. What will my child be learning this year?

2. How will I know if my child has learned it, and how well?

3. How will my child know if he or she has learned it, and how well?

4. What can I do to help my child do well on the specific learning targets taught?

What will my child be learning this year? Increasingly, districts and schools provide information to answer this question. Many districts have developed a comprehensive set of K–12 learning expectations that are aligned to content standards at the state and/or national levels. At this time, 49 of 50 states have developed academic standards, many with the input of teachers, parents, and community members. Many schools have clear and challenging grade-level curricula, designed to help students meet the broader state standards. Further, many districts are making their grade-to-grade curriculum documents available for public review. They have written their curriculum so that each year's learning expectations are connected to what comes before and what comes after. In this way teaching and learning become increasingly sophisticated and challenging as the grade levels increase, aiming at high school graduation competencies. In the fortunate districts where this has already happened, teachers are becoming more purposeful about planning and delivering instruction, and careful consumers of the results of large-scale tests that measure student progress toward them.

How will I know, and how will my child know, if he or she has learned it, and how well? In schools and classrooms where there is no written curriculum, or where it is left on the shelf, there can be no good answer to this second question. It is simply not possible to assess students well or accurately unless the achievement targets students are expected to master have been defined in advance and communicated to them in ways

that they can understand. State standards are not developed to be grade-level curricula; they do not provide adequate guidance to classroom teachers. If the textbook stands in for the curriculum, we encounter one of two dangers: either teachers will be forced to "cover" instead of teach a large portion of the material; or they will select what to teach without an agreed set of priorities. Even with the recent progress in developing curricula in standards-driven systems, too many students come to school wanting to do their best, but without any idea of what they are being asked to learn and why. In states where standards have been established, districts still need to develop a specific, detailed curriculum so that teachers, especially those new to the profession, can know what to teach.

What can I do to help my child do well on the specific learning targets taught? We as parents can help in a number of ways, but all depend on us knowing what our children are learning. First, we can ask our children more specific questions. Rather than ask, "What did you do in school today?", we can ask, "What are you learning in math this week?" With an understandable grade-level curriculum in hand, we can help our children articulate which learning targets represent strengths for them and which they still need to work on. ("I'm getting better at spelling homonyms. Homonyms are words that sound alike but are spelled differently and have different meanings, like *pair* and *pear*.") We are better prepared to help with homework when the intended learning is clear. Think back to Jevon's experience with spelling. His parents know how to focus their involvement with homework: help Jevon practice spelling "long *a* words." If your lives are like ours, you don't have a lot of leisure time on school nights. We all appreciate information that allows us to put effort where it will pay the most dividend.

The Difficulties and Challenges Ahead

Implementing a challenging academic curriculum in every classroom at every grade level is in itself a challenging task for many school districts. Writing specific grade-level curricula to match state standards and selecting or creating classroom assessments to evaluate them requires time and resources at the district level. State standards are often broadly written to cover a range of grade levels; districts must flesh them out to create a usable document for their teachers. In many cases, teachers still need to break down their grade-level or subject area curricula further into smaller teachable and assessable targets. And in the end, teachers decide what is taught in the classroom. The quality of our children's education is affected both by the quality of the curriculum in place and by the extent to which their teachers decide to follow that curriculum.

Teachers as Masters of the Targets

One essential foundation of effective schools is teachers who are confident, competent masters of the targets their students are to master. Research over the last 20 years has shown that the single biggest factor influencing student achievement is the quality of teaching. That quality begins with the teacher's mastery of subject matter knowledge. Once the curriculum is written, it is crucial to quality education that all teachers be masters of the targets they are charged with teaching. Students cannot be expected to learn what teachers themselves do not understand and are therefore not able to teach or assess effectively. With demanding standards now in place in most states, the issue of teachers' subject matter knowledge becomes even more critical to student success. Unfortunately, recent surveys show that many teachers do not think they are receiving adequate support in teaching to the standards, and that much of the professional development they receive is not linked closely enough to content standards.

Chapter 3 — Important Ideas

- School districts need a high-quality written curriculum in place to guide teaching and learning.

- A high-quality written curriculum balances four kinds of learning expectations—knowledge, reasoning, skill, and product—to reflect application of each subject in life beyond school.

- Students learn more when they know what they are expected to achieve. When they know what constitutes quality work, and when teachers directly connect their teaching to those expectations, the probability rises that students will meet the achievement expectations we hold for them.

- When local curriculum is aligned to state standards and teachers follow the local curriculum, students are being prepared to show what they have learned on the state tests, without a lot of external, time-consuming "test prep" activities.

- A curriculum document in everyday language can help you know what children in your district are learning, and it can be useful in knowing how to help your child at home.

- It's okay to ask your local school about the educational background and qualifications of your child's teacher because preparation to teach a particular subject is fundamental to your child's success.

- Our schools need to provide teachers the opportunity to understand the curriculum standards they are given to teach, as well as time to align their lessons to those standards.

Chapter 4

Classroom Assessment: Principles, Methods, and Issues of Quality

When you think about the ways you were tested in school, what images come to mind? Essays in blue books; true or false quizzes; matching columns of names, numbers, and facts; fill-in-the-blank items; and lengthy term papers are pretty common for most of us. Assessment in school today still includes these kinds of tests, but it also includes other experiences we may not have had growing up. In this chapter we'll explain the principles of assessment quality, the variety of assessment methods used in schools today, and the reasons for using each. We'll also give examples of formative assessment and student involvement in the context of classroom assessments. Last, we'll explore how homework fits into the assessment picture and offer guidelines for parent involvement in homework.

Assessment Principles: Standards of Quality

All high-quality assessments adhere to the same basic standards, which can be organized as answers to five questions (Figure 4.1): Why? What? How? How much? How accurate?

Figure 4.1 Five Standards of Quality Assessment

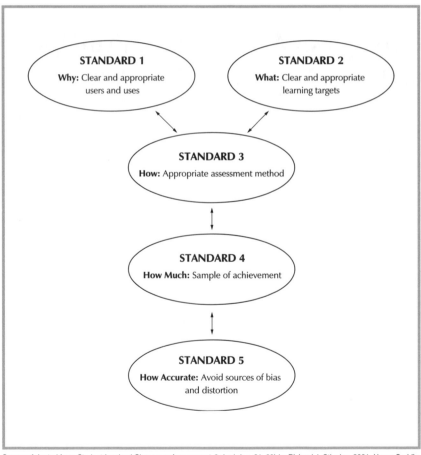

Source: Adapted from *Student-Involved Classroom Assessment*, 3rd ed. (pp. 21, 30) by Richard J. Stiggins, 2001, Upper Saddle River, NJ: Merrill-Prentice Hall. Copyright © 2001 by Prentice-Hall, Inc. Adapted by permission.

Why: Clear and Appropriate Users and Uses

Chapter 2 focused on this first standard of quality. In that chapter, we concluded that the primary purpose of assessment should be to improve student learning. Remember that different kinds of assessments meet the needs of different decision makers. Being clear from the outset about what educational decisions each assessment serves is a critical component of a balanced, effective assessment system. Further, commitment to meeting the needs of the most important decision makers—students, teachers, and parents—is an equally crucial component of a healthy assessment system.

What: Clear and Appropriate Learning Targets

Chapter 3 explored clear learning targets, the second standard of quality. As you recall, high-quality assessment cannot happen without a clear picture of the learning to be assessed. Anyone designing or selecting an assessment must understand the learning targets, or the assessment has little chance of reflecting student achievement of the intended learning.

How: Appropriate Assessment Method

The different kinds of assessments in use in schools fall into different categories: selected response, essay, performance assessment, and personal communication. These four methods are not interchangeable; quality assessment demands that teachers select the method that will provide the best information for the intended purpose and measure the intended learning most accurately. Some assessment methods are a better match than others for certain kinds of learning targets. We illustrate this match in Table 4.1.

Table 4.1 Best Matches Between Learning Targets and Assessment Methods

TARGET TO BE ASSESSED	SELECTED RESPONSE	ESSAY	PERFORMANCE ASSESSMENT	PERSONAL COMMUNICATION
KNOWLEDGE MASTERY	Multiple-choice, true-false, matching, and fill-in items can sample mastery of elements of knowledge	Essay exercises can tap understanding of relationships among elements of knowledge	Not a good choice for this target—three other options preferred	Can ask questions, evaluate answers, and infer mastery, but a time-consuming option
REASONING PROFICIENCY	Can assess application of some patterns of reasoning	Written descriptions of complex problem solutions can provide a window into reasoning proficiency	Can watch students solve some problems or examine some products and infer about reasoning proficiency	Can ask student to "think aloud" or can ask followup questions to probe reasoning
SKILLS	Can assess mastery of the knowledge prerequisites to skillful performance, but cannot rely on these to tap the skill itself		Can observe and evaluate skills as they are being performed	Strong match when skill is oral communication proficiency; also can assess mastery of knowledge prerequisite to skillful performance
ABILITY TO CREATE PRODUCTS	Can assess mastery of the knowledge prerequisite to the ability to create quality products, but cannot use these to assess the quality of products themselves		Can assess both proficiency in carrying out steps in product development, and attributes of the product itself	Can probe procedural knowledge and knowledge of attributes of quality products, but not quality of product

Source: Adapted from *Student-Involved Classroom Assessment*, 3rd ed. (p. 93) by Richard J. Stiggins, 2001, Upper Saddle River, NJ: Merrill-Prentice Hall. Copyright © 2001 by Prentice-Hall, Inc. Adapted by permission.

In addition, there are standards for quality that pertain to each individual method. We don't believe the majority of our readers aspire to be test developers; therefore, we'll share what you in your roles as parents and community members might want and need to know about each method.

How Much: Adequate Sample of Achievement

This standard for quality requires that assessments be designed to gather the right amount of information about the learning to be measured. Does the assessor have enough information to draw confident conclusions about students' achievement on each of the content standards? How much information is enough? These are the questions educators must know how to answer when attending to sampling issues.

How Accurate: Avoid Sources of Bias and Distortion

Everything up to this point can be carried out well—clear purpose, clear targets, appropriate assessment method, and the right amount of information—and things can still go wrong! Results can be made inaccurate in a number of ways. Educators call these *sources of bias and distortion.*

An assessment is considered *biased* when students' scores are altered by factors that don't have a direct connection to the achievement being assessed. Sources of bias include the following (Stiggins 2001):

- Conditions in the assessment environment (a fire alarm during a timed test, missing materials, noise distractions)

- Conditions within the student (lack of reading skill, poor health, lack of test-taking skills, tendency to "freeze" on tests)

- Problems with the assessment itself (vague or missing directions, poorly worded questions, culturally biased questions)

69

It is the teacher's job to identify and eliminate sources of bias and distortion whenever possible, and to use assessment results appropriately or disregard them altogether when there is evidence that the results are inaccurate.

These five standards are used to judge the quality of all forms of assessment. Educators who are assessment literate think through each one as preparation for developing or selecting any assessment they give.

Methods of Assessment

Did you have a favorite type of test or assessment when you were in school? A preference for true-false questions over essay questions, for example? This is what we mean by the term *methods*— the different ways used in school to evaluate learning. There are four basic categories of assessment methods: *selected response, essay, performance assessment,* and *personal communication.* As you read through the explanation of each, think about which of these you have experienced in your school career.

Selected Response Tests

Selected response test items are used to measure students' knowledge and reasoning proficiencies. They have one correct answer or a limited number of correct answers, and may be multiple-choice, matching, fill-in-the-blank or short answer, or true-false questions. Examples of the kinds of learning appropriately assessed by selected response items include knowledge of correct grammar and parts of speech, the structure of the U.S. government, and choosing which operation to use to solve math problems. Standardized tests use this method to a large extent because it is easy to administer and inexpensive to score.

Essay Questions

Essay questions are also used to measure students' knowledge and reasoning proficiencies. To perform well on an essay test question, students must answer the question asked and provide the information required. Each correct response may not look exactly the same, but all correct responses share common characteristics, which depend on the question asked. Responses with some, but not all, of these characteristics receive partial credit. Essay questions are often worth more than one point on a test, to reflect both their relative importance to the test and to allow for partial credit.

Performance Assessment

Performance assessment can be used to measure students' reasoning proficiency, ability to perform skillfully, or ability to create a quality product. Examples of learning targets best measured by performance assessment include giving an oral presentation, writing a research paper, setting up and conducting a science experiment, and properly operating a particular device or tool. In a performance assessment students are given a *task*—an assignment—and *criteria*—requirements that describe the elements of quality needed for the particular performance or product.

For example, your ninth-grade child may be responsible for mastering the following learning target: *The student speaks effectively to various audiences and purposes.* The *task*, or

71

assignment, may be to prepare and deliver a three-minute oral presentation to the class on a specified topic. The *criteria* for judging the quality of the presentation may describe (1) the content, (2) the organization of the content, (3) the delivery— volume, eye contact, and so forth—and (4) the grammar. So, the criteria define what we mean by "speaks effectively." In this case, the expanded description of the criteria would mean the student does the following:

- Selects ideas that are interesting to the audience and important to the topic

- Organizes the ideas logically, with an inviting introduction and a satisfying conclusion

- Delivers the speech with appropriate voice volume, rate, and articulation

- Uses actions (arm movements, walking around) to enhance meaning

- Uses correct pronunciation and grammar

Personal Communication

Personal communication is another way to determine students' knowledge and reasoning proficiencies. This method of assessment is just what it seems: the teacher asks a question or engages in a dialogue with the student, and listens to determine the quality of the responses. Assessments in the primary grades rely heavily on this one-on-one method.

Table 4.2 presents examples of each of the four assessment methods.

Table 4.2 The Four Assessment Methods

METHOD	WHAT IT MEASURES	EXAMPLES
SELECTED RESPONSE	**KNOWLEDGE** Learning Target: Knows why United States was colonized	Why did colonists migrate to the United States? a. To escape taxation b. For religious freedom c. For adventure d. More than one of the above (Stiggins 2001, p. 139)
	Learning Target: Identifies placement of instruments in an orchestra	In what section of the orchestra is the kettle drum found? _____ (Stiggins 2001, p. 142)
	REASONING Learning Target: Infers	As employment increases, the danger of inflation increases. a. True, because consumers are willing to pay higher prices b. True, because the money supply increases c. False, because wages and inflation are statistically unrelated to one another d. False, because the government controls inflation (Stiggins 2001, p. 142)
	REASONING Learning Target: Classifies	Given what you know about animal life of the arid, temperate, and arctic regions, if you found an animal with the following characteristics, in which region would you expect it to live? (A description of the animal's characteristics is inserted here.) a. arid region b. temperate region c. arctic region (Stiggins 2001, p. 285)

Table 4.2 The Four Assessment Methods *(Continued)*

METHOD	WHAT IT MEASURES	EXAMPLES
ESSAY	**KNOWLEDGE** Learning Target: Understands the water cycle	Describe how evaporation and condensation operate in the context of the water cycle. Be sure to include all key elements in the cycle and how they relate to one another. (Stiggins 2001, p. 163)
	REASONING Learning Target: Evaluates	Some argue for and some against irrigating deserts to grow food. Take a position on this issue and defend it. Make explicit the criteria you are using as the basis for your position and be sure to apply them logically. (Stiggins 2001, p. 287)
PERFORMANCE ASSESSMENT	**REASONING** Learning Target: Uses scientific thinking process to conduct investigations	Task: Students are presented with two seemingly identical glasses of soda, but one is the diet version. They are to identify which is which. Criteria: The teacher observes as each student proceeds, and uses criteria to evaluate the student's level of proficiency with applying the scientific method. (Stiggins 2001, p. 288)
	SKILL Learning Target: Reads aloud with fluency	Task: Student reads text aloud. Criteria: Teacher listens as each student reads and uses criteria to evaluate the student's level of oral reading fluency.

Table 4.2 The Four Assessment Methods *(Continued)*

METHOD	WHAT IT MEASURES	EXAMPLES
PERFORMANCE ASSESSMENT *(Continued)*	**PRODUCT** Learning Target: Writes a compare/contrast essay	Task: Students write an essay that compares and contrasts major advantages and disadvantages of three forms of business: proprietorships, partnerships, and corporations. Criteria: Teacher uses criteria that describe a quality compare/contrast paper to evaluate the essay. Criteria focus on content and organization of the ideas.
PERSONAL COMMUNICATION	**KNOWLEDGE** Learning Target: Knows the steps of the writing process	Teacher asks individual students to explain the steps of the writing process.
	REASONING Learning Target: Draws conclusions	Teacher asks individual students to explain why a conclusion is correct or incorrect.
	SKILL Learning Target: Uses communication strategies and skills to work effectively with others	Task: Students are given a problem to solve as a group. Criteria: Teacher observes group interactions and evaluates each individual's performance using criteria that reflect effective communication skills, e.g., acknowledges others' points of view, makes individual contributions, extends the contributions of others.

75

Which Method Is Best?

There is no one "best" assessment method; each one can be used well or poorly. The method used depends, for the most part, on the kind of learning target to be assessed. Let's look at a few examples of this idea.

Suppose the list of learning expectations for your child's second-year Spanish course includes the ability to speak Spanish conversationally in a limited set of contexts, such as when asking directions, purchasing items, and conversing with a host family. Could the teacher assess your child's achievement on this learning target with a multiple-choice test? With an essay question? The answer to both of these questions is "No." A multiple-choice or fill-in-the-blank item could test students' knowledge of vocabulary, which is certainly necessary to holding a conversation. In an essay question, the students could write out their part of the dialogue; knowing what to say is also necessary to the conversation. However, if the learning target calls for students to *speak conversationally*, they must actually engage in a conversation in Spanish to demonstrate the extent to which they have mastered this learning target. The teacher must use a performance assessment to get the achievement information.

Without information provided by selected response and essay tests, we may not get an accurate picture of the knowledge base and reasoning proficiencies we want our children to have. Yet we know the purpose of education is not to master content purely for the sake of knowing it. We want our children to be able to apply that knowledge to contexts and situations they will encounter in life beyond school, whether they choose to venture into further education or the job market. Therefore, students must have opportunities to learn how to perform skillfully with knowledge and to demonstrate their achievements in our K–12 schools. That calls for performance assessment.

As an example, read through this partial list of learning targets for an elementary school science unit, "The Physics of Sound," and think about how each might be assessed:

1. Learn vocabulary associated with the physics of sound.

2. Understand that sound is produced by vibrating objects.

3. Understand the relationship between the pitch of a sound and the physical properties of the sound source (i.e., length of vibrating object, frequency of vibrations, and tension of vibrating string).

4. Compare methods to amplify sound at the source and at the receiver.

5. Use scientific thinking processes to conduct investigations and build explanations: observing, communicating, comparing, and organizing.

A teacher who wants to assess students' achievement on these learning targets will have to use more than one assessment method. The first three learning targets could be measured accurately and efficiently with selected response test items. The fourth learning target could be measured well either with selected response test items or with an essay question. The last learning target asks students to conduct investigations and create explanations, which requires performance assessment.

Issues of Quality

Selected Response Tests

We often think of selected response testing as the traditional, tried-and-true method of assessment. Most of us are familiar with it. Did you know that in the 1930s and 1940s selected response tests were the wave of the future, only used in the classroom by the most progressive teachers? Far from being tried and true, they were the innovation; the traditional methods before this scientific breakthrough were essay and performance assessment. Most of us also regard selected response tests as *objective*, because the scoring is straightforward: an answer is either right or wrong. That much is true; the scoring is the objective part.

However, selected response testing is just as subjective as any other method. Subjectivity comes in when choosing what to put on the test that most closely matches the intended learning. Selected content might vary because the actual instruction varies from class to class, depending on the curriculum, as well as on the prior knowledge and interests of the particular group of students. Therefore, test content must vary accordingly, if it is to measure what students are responsible for learning.

Even though selecting test content is somewhat subjective, there are limits to legitimate choices. Have you ever taken a test and wondered why in the world the teacher included a certain question? Or encountered an item representing trivia from the caption of an illustration in the text? The questions on the test should relate directly to the main content categories and patterns of reasoning taught. When a selected response test is carried out well, the general content of the test comes as no surprise to the attentive student.

The individual items on a selected response test must also adhere to standards of quality. Well-written questions maximize the chances that students who know the information get them right and students who do not know the information get them wrong. Well-written questions should indicate who knows the information and who doesn't.

Let's look at an experience one of the authors (Steve) had as a student, to illustrate two problems with selected response test quality:

> I remember sitting in a university class completing a matching test where we were asked to select the letter in front of one word in the righthand column and place it in the blank in front of a phrase in the lefthand column. I noticed that if I read down the left column, the letters in the answer blanks spelled out predictable words and phrases. A few other students had figured out the same thing and were nervously glancing around, smiling, and shaking their heads in disgust. I exited that class with a distrust of tests, and for a short time, looked for hidden tricks on subsequent tests. The most frustrating part, however, was the low level of knowledge required to do well on the test, even without the predictable answer pattern. I'd prepared to demonstrate a deeper level of competence, certain I was going to have to write, explain myself, and defend my answers. This was not an opportunity to demonstrate what I had learned—it was a meaningless exercise.

Steve's university experience illustrates two problems, one with test content and the other with item writing. He encountered a basic knowledge test, which did not match or measure the level of learning expected from the course. And, anyone who figured out the pattern of correct responses could have scored highly on the test without having learned the content. The instructor would have had equally valid information to use for course grades if he had just thrown the numbers in the air and randomly assigned them. Even if the items had been written correctly, because of the content mismatch the test would still have been a waste of everyone's time and university resources.

Performance Assessment

High-quality performance assessment requires that students clearly understand both the *task*—the assignment—and the *criteria*—the description of quality they are to aim for. Let's look to a problem from the other author's (Jan's) classroom teaching experience to highlight issues of quality in a simple performance assessment:

> One year while teaching sixth grade, I held a sched-uled conference with a parent who questioned a report card grade of "C" I had given her son in handwriting. I explained it by saying his handwriting was readable, but he was not forming his letters very well. Her response hit home. She delivered it politely, but the gist of it was, "How can you grade something you don't teach? How did you determine his grade was a 'C' in handwrit-ing? How does my son know what's expected? Does he have opportunity to practice to get better in class? If he's supposed to practice at home, does he know what to do?"

Although a handwriting grade might seem somewhat insignif-icant, the incident points out serious problems that can be lurking in any performance assessment. The first has to do with learning targets. We sixth-grade teachers were required to grade handwriting on the report card, but we had no curriculum saying

what to teach, and no materials to teach or assess it. We should have questioned this, but we didn't. The parent, however, rightly did.

The second problem gets more to issues of performance assessment quality. Handwriting, as with most other products or skills we judge with performance assessment, cannot be marked right or wrong—there is no answer key for grading it. It requires a description of quality. These descriptions of quality are commonly called *criteria, rubrics*, or *scoring guides*. To establish criteria for evaluating handwriting, first we would need to differentiate levels of quality—"Excellent," "Acceptable," "Close to Acceptable," and "Needs Major Work," for example. Then we would need to create a separate description for each level. What does excellent handwriting look like? What does acceptable (or "adequate" or "meets the standard") handwriting look like? We cannot evaluate handwriting, or any skill or product, fairly without such a scale of descriptions.

A third problem arises when we don't have samples of quality at each level, both for the assessors to use when they make their judgments, and also for students as they prepare their work. The student who received a "C" in handwriting benefits as a learner when he can (1) see examples of good and not-so-good handwriting, (2) match his own handwriting to an example to see where he is now, and (3) work with his teacher to set goals for improvement.

What to Look for

Although it is not our job as parents and community members to audit classroom assessments for quality, there are certain things we can keep an eye out for without needing to be test development experts. We can check for balance. Does the teacher use more than one assessment method? Or, are all assessments of one kind (all selected response tests, or all performance assessments)? This is not always cause for concern, but it should cause us to look more closely at the learning targets. We can look for commonsense matches between assessment method and learning targets. For example, in mathematics, the ability to select and implement a strategy to solve a problem is an important learning target. So, in mathematics classes, we should see evidence of performance assessment, where students must choose and use an appropriate strategy to solve specific problems. We can also ask if the collection of assessments conducted during the year reflects all of the important aspects of the target. If the learning target is "writes coherently," do the assessments only test for correct grammar, spelling, capitalization, and punctuation? Or, is student writing also evaluated for other important elements of quality, such as ideas and content, organization, and word choice?

Formative Assessment and Student Involvement Within Each Assessment Method

Each assessment method—selected response, essay, performance assessment, and personal communication—can be used in a summative way to measure achievement at the end of learning. Each can also be used diagnostically, as a pretest, to determine specific learning needs in advance of teaching. But if our goal is to improve student learning, each must be used formatively in the classroom as well, to promote achievement *during* learning. What does that look like for students in the classroom?

First, teachers explain the learning targets in ways that help students understand what they are expected to know and be able to do. For example, today, from 9:00 to 9:45, your fourth grader is learning math, or more specifically, decimals. To be exact, the class is working on page 152 in their math books. At the outset of the lesson, your son's teacher tells the class, "Today we will be learning how to read and compare decimals. We arc going to learn how to say them correctly and how to put them in order from least to greatest and greatest to least."

Second, students discuss models of performance so that they understand the level of achievement they are to aim for. For example, in preparation to write a science experiment report, eighth graders are reading various examples of hypotheses (from a similar, but different, experiment), discussing them, and using a scoring guide to evaluate them for the characteristics of a good hypothesis. They then write a short description in their own words of what a good hypothesis does.

83

Third, students understand the assessment plan—when and how each learning target will be assessed, and how the information will be used (for diagnostic, formative, or summative purposes). For example, at the beginning of a unit on the Civil War, tenth-grade students receive a calendar that lists the learning targets for the unit, shows when each will be assessed, and indicates the purpose for each assessment event—diagnostic, formative, or summative. These purposes are explained to students as "pretest," "progress check," and "for a grade."

Fourth, students have opportunities to practice, receive feedback, and use that feedback to improve their learning, before the summative assessment. For example, in a seventh-grade literature class, one of the learning targets is to compare and contrast characters from two different texts. The teacher has decided to assign a compare–contrast paper as part of a summative assessment. Along the way, students will write a shorter compare–contrast paper, receive specific feedback from both teacher and peers regarding strengths and weaknesses, and revise their papers based on that feedback.

Fifth, students learn to identify their own strengths and set goals for improvement, using specific terms relating directly to the intended learning targets. For example, fifth-grade students review their progress in reading comprehension by looking through a portfolio of their recent assignments. The collection includes evidence of their ability to summarize text, interpret unfamiliar vocabulary, and make inferences and predictions based on the reading. Here's an excerpt from a student's reflection on her learning: "I have learned how to make inferences this quarter. An inference is where you figure out something that the story suggests, but doesn't say outright. I used to just guess, but now I look for clues in the story. For next quarter I am going to work on writing summaries. I am going

84

to work on only including the most important information. My summaries have too much extra stuff in them."

These five steps illustrate the practices advocated by Black and Wiliam (1998) and introduced in Chapter 2 as being so powerful in bringing about higher levels of achievement. Think back to the oral presentation example described earlier. Now imagine yourself as a ninth grader learning how to give oral presentations. If you are like the majority of us, this is not a pleasant thought. But what if, rather than being given the assignment and some time to prepare individually, you had the opportunity to go through the five steps discussed here? Chances are, you would have felt more in control of the conditions of your success and more confident when it came your turn to get up in front of the audience. Chances are also good that you would have performed well.

Helping with Homework

Homework is one of the constants in our lives as parents—a direct connection between school and home that provides us a glimpse of what our children are learning. As schools raise standards and high-stakes tests become more common, many teachers and schools are increasing the amount of homework assigned as a way of helping students perform better on state tests. Increased homework requires increased vigilance on our part as parents in ensuring it is assigned for the right purpose and is matched to students' needs, abilities, and ages. Many schools and districts have policies that spell out the purpose of homework, provide guidelines on the amount of homework to be assigned, and explain the basis for evaluating homework and its relationship to calculating report card grades. We deal with the report card issue in more detail in Chapter 6.

In the end, it's likely that for every parent who thinks there's too much homework there's another who thinks there isn't enough. But as with so many things, it is the kind of homework, rather than the amount, that counts.

The Purpose of Homework

Recently, our daughter was assigned a task to be completed at home—the Pet Project, in which she was to collect and display on a poster interesting facts about her cat. Our first thoughts were, "What can we do to help her?" Or, put another way, "How can we avoid a late night the evening before it's due?"

To know what help is appropriate, we need to know the assignment's purpose. The teacher can include a note to parents explaining why students are doing the task, or students can write the note themselves, thereby increasing the chances that both they and their parents understand the reason. When parental help is not appropriate, it is still critical that students understand the reason for the assignment and see a link to the important learning targets for the class.

Homework has many legitimate purposes (Guskey 2002b):

- To practice skills presented that day

- To give students time to conduct independent research

- To review notes in preparation for future work or assessments

- To develop research and study techniques

- To foster self-discipline and responsibility

A secondary goal of homework can be to increase communication between school and home. It can serve to inform us about what students are learning, especially when assignments involve us in the work. For example, students may be required to interview parents, they may be assigned a topic to explore in tandem with a parent, or parents may be asked, as a part of the assignment, to check students' work (Guskey 2002b). These opportunities allow us to let our children know how important their work is to us.

Whatever the purpose, parents and students both need to know the assignment's goal.

Productive Homework Help

On any homework, what support is most productive? It can be as simple as valuing homework by making sure sufficient time is set aside each evening, without other activities interfering. In doing so, we communicate that homework is part of the responsibility of learning. Or, support can be as "hands on" as showing your child how to "solve for *X*." Whether or not the purpose or parameters for your involvement come home with the assignment, there are several steps you can take to get the most out of homework time at your house.

Consider the purpose for the homework. This will help both you and your child know what kind of help will be most in keeping with the reason the teacher assigned the homework in the first place. If it is not obvious from the assignment, ask, or have your child ask the teacher for an explanation—a polite version of, "Why are we doing this?" ("Because I said so" may stand in for an answer at home, but it is not sufficient in the case of homework.)

Ensure understanding of the learning expectations. You can ask if your child understands the intended learning—"I am doing this project to learn _____." If he or she isn't clear, and you can't figure it out from what comes home, encourage your child to ask the teacher for clarification. Children can direct their own work much better if they understand the intended learning targets.

Plan your help accordingly. Information about purpose and learning expectations will guide your decisions about what help to give. For example, if our daughter's teacher intends to use the Pet Project mentioned previously as evidence of our child's ability to choose interesting details to share, we may help her think of what is most interesting or unusual about Bob the cat, but we'll be careful not to supply the details for her. If she is to use her gathered facts as the text for an oral presentation, we may suggest she practice using the information on her poster as talking points, and we may help her rehearse.

Don't over-help. Then, we need to be careful not to over-help. Projects—or any homework—provide us an opportunity to work with our children, but we need to be aware of the goal of the assignment. If, for example our daughter's teacher assigned the Pet Project as a report, chances are she has assigned it to help students become better writers. We must be vigilant in asking ourselves, "Is the goal to produce good writing or to produce a good writer?" If the goal of the Pet Project is to produce good writing, we should get the child out of the way, because we (in theory, anyway) can do it better without her. And then let's be honest about who did the work! (If we contribute to the assignment, we should identify the work that is ours so the teacher doesn't think it represents what our child knows. Even if the work would get a higher grade with our contributions, our child won't be proud of what she didn't do.) On the other hand, if the goal of the Pet Project is to produce a good writer, then we must let our daughter do the work. The person who holds the pencil does the learning.

The Homework–Assessment Connection

Remember, the kind of help we give, should our children want or need it, is governed by the reason for the homework. Is it to practice what they learned in class? This use of homework can help students remember concepts and skills introduced in the lesson that day. If your children are struggling with homework that is practice, it's fine to help them, or show them how to do it, without doing the work for them. To maintain the integrity of their work and their sense of accomplishment, we can encourage our children to mark the problems we helped with: "I did ten of these by myself and two of them with help from my dad." (We got this idea from our daughter, whose first spoken phrase in life was, "Do by self.") It also provides good feedback to the teacher regarding how well students understood the day's lessons.

When homework is for practice, students should receive timely feedback on the assignment that lets them know what they did well and what they need to work on. Otherwise, what is the contribution of homework to learning? In general, such assignments should not be figured into the report card grade. Factoring every piece of work, including the practice pieces, into the final grade penalizes the student who has much to learn, and learns it! (We take up this topic further in Chapter 6.)

Sometimes teachers assign tasks as homework that they will use as formative assessment. If this is the case, tread lightly in the helping department. When the purpose of the assignment is to gather information about students' achievement to plan further instruction or to have students self-assess, the work needs to be their own.

If the homework is a summative assessment, a term paper for instance, it is especially important to know what assistance is allowed. Then, beyond the parameters of what is allowed, our helping stance needs to be "hands off." Our children do not become better learners (or honest citizens) when we do work for them. Besides, we parents already had our shot at eleventh-grade English—it's their turn. In situations such as the term paper, productive help consists of making sure our children have access to the resources they need and guaranteeing undisturbed homework time in the evenings.

Chapter 4 — Important Ideas

- Educators who are assessment literate use five standards of quality to plan and give any assessment. They determine the purpose, clarify the targets, select the method, sample appropriately, and control for bias and distortion.

- When classroom assessment is done well, teachers use an array of methods, depending on the learning targets to be assessed. They consider which method will give the most accurate picture of student achievement on the particular learning targets, and also which method will be most efficient, that is, which will take the least amount of time.

- Each assessment method can and should be used formatively, to increase students' understanding of the achievement expectations and to build their confidence as learners.

- When helping with homework, we need to keep the purpose for the homework in mind. We as parents can play a productive part in homework completion, but we must be careful not to over-help.

Chapter 5

Standardized Testing

Do you have any idea how many assessments you took in your school career? Realistically, none of us probably does. If we tried to count them, we'd have to include not just the big tests but also the daily math quizzes, the weekly spelling test, the end-of-chapter questions, and all of the other ways our teachers assessed how well we were learning. An assessment event happens for every student in every classroom multiple times per week, if not per day. It's fair to say that over 99 percent of any student's assessment experiences occur in the classroom with teacher-made tests and assessments, scored and graded in mostly traditional, familiar ways.

And yet the other testing, the external, large-scale standardized assessment *of* learning, the part of testing that makes up less than 1 percent of the assessment record of any student, captures 99 percent of public and media attention, and 100 percent of the political and policy discussion. And unfortunately, with that attention comes the mistaken notion that somehow these tests can provide more meaningful and accurate data about student learning than that generated in the classroom. The fact is, the further away testing gets from the classroom (school, district, state, national, international) the less can be known and reported that is meaningful about individual students. Still, this has not slowed our national obsession with using standardized test results to compare, judge, reward, sanction, promote, certify, validate, and criticize. Holding our schools accountable for higher test scores and giving those scores to teachers for instructional planning do not meet the teachers' need for information about student achievement.

In this chapter we'll look at the standardized tests that make up that small percentage of evidence of student learning, tests that continue to play an even larger role in education in America. What are we as parents and community members to make of the information provided? Is any of it useful to us? We'll answer these questions by explaining the meaning of the scores, the purposes for which they are designed, and appropriate uses of the information they provide. We also readdress the question, "Why do we have so many standardized tests?" It's important to emphasize that we are not opposed to standardized testing. Many of these tests can and do provide useful information to parents and educators. But remember, they are primarily designed to inform policy-level decisions about the effectiveness of schools.

Even though these tests can contribute to school improvement, we remain concerned by their overuse in measuring and reporting student learning. Real learning and understanding cannot and should not be trivialized into a single score. Once-a-year, standardized tests "are not likely to be of much specific value to classroom teachers. They are too infrequent, broad in focus, and slow in returning results to inform the ongoing array of day-to-day decisions" (Stiggins 2001, p. 376). We believe that until we acknowledge the limitations of these tests and bring classroom assessment into a more balanced partnership with large-scale standardized assessments *of* learning we will not fully ensure the accuracy and quality of information coming home about student learning.

What Is a Standardized Test?

The word *standardized* simply means that the same set of test questions is given the same way and under exactly the same conditions to all students. Further, all tests are scored the same way. Each student taking the test has the same time limitations and follows the same set of directions. It is this commonality and consistency of test administration that gives all scores exactly the same meaning, which, in turn allows individual and group scores to be compared to one another.

Additionally, standardized test scores can be broken out to monitor and report achievement by student subgroups. This is one way schools track fairness or equity in education—by looking at scores separated according to gender, ethnicity, socioeconomic status, and participation in special programs, such as special education. Districts do this to identify gaps among subgroups; if boys consistently score higher than girls in science, for example, the district may take certain actions to address the disparity.

Standardized tests widely used at the district level are often designed to cover the academic content of more than one year on any given test. Therefore, the tests reflect broad achievement targets. Because the number of items on a test is limited, there may be only 12 items representing a year's learning in that subject. The reason for this relates to the purpose of the test: to make broad statements about what students know and can do in order to compare groups to each other. The goal of large-scale standardized tests is *not* to gather information

for individual student instructional planning.

Often standardized test scores can be broken down according to the specific learning targets assessed. This data must be used carefully, because there may not be enough questions covering any one learning target to truly measure student proficiency on that one target. To compensate for this, most test results are broken down into clusters of learning targets, such as "Spelling" (as opposed to "spells words with the long *a* sound"), or "Grammar" (as opposed to "uses subject and object pronouns correctly") on a language arts subtest. Such information is most useful when a school staff is identifying areas needing extra attention in a particular subject, but it is limited by its lack of specificity.

The kind of standardized tests most often selected for district-level testing programs measure knowledge and reasoning learning targets. Skill and product targets are not represented on the majority of them (Stiggins & Knight 1997). In such cases, judging the quality of schools on the basis of these test scores alone is risky.

Standardized test results can seem like gobbledygook, but once you understand a few basic concepts, you will know what it is you are reading when your child brings results home and will be able to ask specific questions of your school to get the information you want. Standardized tests come in two basic "flavors," norm referenced and criterion referenced. These terms refer to two different ways the results of the test are interpreted and presented. We'll explain a bit about each one to give you the information you need to be an informed consumer who makes intelligent use of the data they produce.

Norm-Referenced Standardized Test Scores

Percent Correct and Percentile

Norm-referenced standardized tests interpret students' scores by comparing them to the scores of other students (the *norm group*). You know your child has taken a norm-referenced test if the results are reported as *percentile* scores: "Your child scored at the 72nd *percentile* (also written as %ile) in math." What does this score mean? How is this different from scoring 72 *percent* on a test? The difference lies in what a *percentile* is and how it is computed.

First, let's briefly review how a *percent* score (which we'll call a *percent correct* score) is calculated. To get a percent correct score, just as you'd imagine, the number of correct answers is divided by the number of questions on the test. For example, a typical classroom math test may have a possible correct score of 30. Any student who scores 30 points on that test answered all of the questions correctly and gets 100 percent. Let's say a student answers 25 of the 30 correctly. In that case the student's percent correct score would be 25 divided by 30—or 83 percent. You may be familiar with this score because teachers often use percent correct scores on their classroom assessments to indicate a student's level of achievement of the material taught.

But norm-referenced standardized tests serve a different purpose than classroom assessments. In this case, tests are designed to compare students and, when averaged across students, to compare schools or even districts. So their scores are computed differently—as *percentiles*. It is important that we understand how percent correct and percentile differ. *Percent correct* refers to the percentage of questions the student answered correctly and *percentile* to the percentage of the norm group the student outscored. A student who receives a percentile score of 50 on a standardized math test did not get half of the items right. That would be a percent correct score (10 correct answers divided by 20 possible points equals 50 percent correct). Instead, it means she outscored 50 percent of the students who took the test during what is called the norming process, discussed in the next subsection. To understand this difference, we need to look at how percentiles are calculated.

Percentiles and Test Norming

Standardized norm-referenced test developers (usually very large test publishing companies) write lots of questions to use for each test. They then try out the questions on groups of students (at the same grade level as the test is intended for) to see which ones are really hard, which ones are really easy, and which ones are hard for some students, but not for others. From all those they tried out, they select questions for the real test so they include a balance of each kind of item—hard, easy, and mid-range. They look for questions that differentiate between those who do and do not know the material. From this narrowed-down pool of questions, they build the final test. Then they give this new "trial version" of the test to a large group of students selected to represent the ethnic, socioeconomic, geographic, gender, and cultural profiles of students likely to take the test. This large group is called the *norm group*.

Test developers then analyze the norm group performance. Let's say the possible number right for this particular test is 30. (That means there were 30 questions, or the points for each question on the test added up to 30.) *Each student's percentile score is determined by how many students in the norm group scored lower than that student did.* For example, let's say a student got 25 questions right out of 30, and by so doing, outscored 92 percent of the norm group students taking the test. The raw score of 25 becomes a percentile score of 92. This is how percentile scores are figured for each raw score. A student who scored 26 right, for example, outscored more norm group students than a student who got just 25 right. So that student's percentile score will be higher. For any normed test, the norm group takes the test once and their scores are spread out over a scale from 1 to 99. That scale becomes the percentile scale to which each subsequent student's score is compared.

No test, not even an expensive, carefully developed test, is perfect in determining student achievement. All tests contain a little bit of "error." This is because test questions are imperfect, the sample of questions put on a test can be biased to some extent, and students can just have a bad day. For this reason, an individual student's *true score* lies within a range of points. This range is known as the *margin of error* for that particular test. Test developers use a formula to determine how accurate the results are when reported for an individual or as a group average. To understand this, think of what happens with political opinion polling. The results are always reported with a margin of error of plus or minus a certain number

of points. Test scores must be interpreted in this same way. Your child's 72nd percentile score on the math test actually represents a midpoint in a range of scores that could also represent your child's achievement. You can find that range on the score report you receive. It is reported as plus or minus a certain number of points.

The accuracy of information from these tests increases when the data are averaged for a number of individuals. The more individual student scores the average percentile score represents, the smaller the margin of error and the more likely the data are to be an accurate picture of what students know about the content on the test.

Grade-Level Equivalent Scores

A grade-level equivalent score often accompanies other scores on an individual student's standardized test report. This norm-referenced score translates student performance to years and months. For example, your third grader may have a grade-level equivalent score on a reading test of 5.5, meaning fifth grade, fifth month. It does not compare your child's reading achievement to any preset standard for what should be learned in fifth grade. It doesn't mean that your child is capable of, or should be doing, fifth-grade work. It means she is doing third-grade work as well as a fifth grader would do third-grade work. It's another way of saying your child is doing really well in third grade compared to other students.

Limitations of Norm-Referenced Standardized Testing

Norm-referenced tests typically provide percentile scores for content areas such as reading, math, and English usage. While these scores suffice for annual program decisions such as resource allocation or the selection of large-scale instructional packages, both students and teachers need deeper, more complex evidence of achievement because of the more refined nature of the decisions they face. Most norm-referenced standardized tests measure only a limited number of the achievement expectations that we hold as valuable for our students. Their coverage is limited to those expectations that can be assessed with the most efficient of test formats within very narrow time limits in order to minimize testing costs. Typically, the more complex expectations, such as multistage problem solving or performance skills, are left out of annual testing because of the extremely high cost of assessing large numbers of students.

And yet, teachers today are under enormous pressure to raise their students' test scores. Unfortunately, teachers who strive to raise test scores covering a limited range of expectations may narrow their teaching to those targets, thereby neglecting more complex, equally important learning. If students are to be "prepared" for a test, we'd want that preparation to be an ongoing part of classroom instructional practice aimed at increasing learning, rather than have preparation be a superficial, isolated event designed simply to improve the test scores. A test-driven curriculum, where the only things taught are those on the test, is simply a "get rich quick" approach to higher test scores that ends up sacrificing real learning in the classroom.

In the end, what is most important to realize about the large-scale tests or assessments *of* learning is that each test needs to match the purpose for which it was originally developed. Asking any of them to pull double or even triple duty in terms of the intended uses of their results puts the accuracy of the results at risk. Helping make accountability decisions about schools or districts, *and* certifying individual achievement levels for the purpose of graduation, *and* informing classroom instruction about individual students is simply more than any one test can reliably deliver.

Appropriate Uses of Norm-Referenced Test Results

So what are norm-referenced standardized tests good for? They were initially, and are still today, designed to sort students along a continuum of achievement. Norm-referenced standardized tests produce a rank order of achievers from highest to lowest. They work well as tests of certain basic skills and when comparisons of one student to other students are useful. Norm-referenced test scores function as one piece of information that can be used along with other data to place students into special programs. The comparison feature of the score allows educators to determine who is in greatest need of the often limited services. Many states use them to assess system performance. Some accountability systems require dependable evidence of achievement that is comparable across classrooms. This can be gathered using standardized tests. And in the hands of teachers and principals who are assessment literate, they can help educators to learn more about a school's instructional strengths and weaknesses, leading to plans for improving the school that can result in better learning for students.

Criterion-Referenced Standardized Tests

As with norm-referenced standardized tests, when we call a test *criterion referenced*, we are referring to how the results are reported. With criterion-referenced standardized tests, rather than comparing each student's raw score (number of correct answers or points earned) to the performance of the norm group, each student's raw score is compared with a preset standard of acceptable performance, called a *criterion*. The score is typically reported in terms such as "Exceeds the Standard," "Meets the Standard," or "Does Not Meet the Standard." We'll discuss the communications challenges these terms present in Chapter 6.

Criterion-referenced tests are often designed differently than norm-referenced tests. They are usually developed to reflect student attainment of a specific set of learning expectations for a given year in content areas such as mathematics, science, or writing. Typically, these tests provide greater detail about student achievement, going beyond content and reasoning to include skill and product targets. Students may be required to solve and explain a multistep mathematics problem, to conduct a scientific investigation, or to produce an extended writing sample. Each of these tests is scored with a set of criteria (also called a *scoring guide* or *rubric*) developed specifically to define levels of quality for the targeted skill or product. (These criteria are often available to the public online from the state office of education.)

Many states are now using criterion-referenced (sometimes called *standards-based*) tests in combination with norm-referenced tests in their statewide testing programs, linking them to the state learning expectations. By combining these two different types of tests, states have tried to balance and expand the different types of learning targets being assessed for accountability purposes. Most often, norm-referenced tests are used to report on basic knowledge and reasoning learning expectations, and criterion-referenced tests to report on more complex reasoning, skill, and product expectations.

Using Standardized Tests When the Stakes Are High

Recently, we have seen a national surge to use standardized test results to make "high-stakes" decisions—tying important decisions about students, teachers, and schools to the test results. For students this could mean a decision regarding promotion or retention, mandatory course selections, or even graduation. For schools not attaining expected achievement levels, typical consequences include the withholding of funds, teacher or principal reassignment, school reorganization, or in some cases, school closure. Additionally, a few states and districts now link student test scores to pay increases for teachers and administrators.

The use of tests for high-stakes decisions continues to spark controversy. The motivation behind linking such decisions to standardized test results is one we all share: the desire to help students learn at higher levels. The idea behind the link, however, that the threat of failure will cause the students, teachers, and administrators to work harder and do better, is based on the assumption that the only thing required for higher achievement is harder work.

As we have discussed, it is not that simple. When we know what standardized test results can and can't tell us, and when we know about their limitations, we will exercise caution in basing any important decision with far-reaching effects on just one piece of evidence. And so we must look with caution at the current nationwide move towards high-stakes testing.

Specific Concerns About High-Stakes Testing

Those questioning the use of tests in high-stakes situations are concerned about three things: unintended negative effects on students, the extent to which the assessments are capable of delivering precise enough information, and overlimiting the curriculum.

High-stakes decision making based on standardized test scores has a very real potential to harm student learning in several important ways. It may serve to raise, not lower, dropout rates. This is particularly worrisome for some special-needs students, who may have little reason to stay in school if they aren't allowed to graduate until they master all state content standards. Although as a nation, from the highest levels of government to the kindergarten class down the street, we aspire to "leave no child behind," performing badly over and over again in high-stakes testing situations can be the catalyst for ensuring that we will indeed leave behind the very students we hope to help. Those who repeatedly perform poorly are in danger of giving up, and we will have failed to help them, again. Today's tests may be different but the result will be the same as when the explicit goal of testing was to sort and select—to identify and single out the cream of the crop.

In addition, opponents of using standardized tests for high-stakes decisions argue that one set of results does not yield sufficient information to make those sorts of decisions, particularly about individual students. Reducing what has happened over a period of years in the classroom among teachers and learners to a single test score often obscures rather than illuminates learning. Most standardized test scores are too imprecise to inform most kinds of high-stakes decisions. In part this is because some sources of measurement error lay beyond the control of even the very best test makers. So on retesting, a student's score may vary up or down by as much as two years in grade equivalents due to random error alone. Thus, there is the danger that some users will ascribe to test scores a far greater level of precision than is justified, leading to potentially inappropriate decisions.

This is especially alarming when it isn't clear that all students being judged have been uniformly exposed to the learning opportunities that come with a quality curriculum, competent master teachers, and the time and resources necessary to provide extra help when needed. Students may not even be exposed to the academic content at the same time or duration during the school year.

And finally, critics argue that high-stakes testing will serve to narrow the curriculum, a problem described earlier in this chapter. When teachers teach to the tested items the movement towards a comprehensive and balanced standards-based curriculum is undermined; the full range of the standards is sacrificed to devote more time to what will be tested.

Still, although we advocate the use of student-involved classroom assessment as a vehicle for improving student achievement, we are not attempting to eliminate the use of standardized tests. We do, however, believe that parents, educators, community members, and students must be aware that at the least the results from these tests can be misapplied and at the worst they have the potential to do great harm in high-stakes situations.

Chapter 5 — Important Ideas

- Tests designed to serve an accountability purpose by publicly reporting student achievement should not be confused with tests used to improve daily teaching and learning at the classroom level. Nor should they be mistaken for assessments that motivate and inspire confidence for all students.

- Parents should be mindful of the type of test being administered and the intended purpose communicated by the district or the state. If it is designed to be a norm-referenced test, it may not do a good job of measuring progress toward standards.

- More than ever, we need to ensure that teachers and principals know and understand what achievement expectations are assessed on each of these tests and how to interpret and use the resulting scores to improve schools. We face the possibility of the unintentional misuse of results, avoidable only if users are trained to use results effectively. Users in schools and classrooms have not been given the opportunity to develop those understandings.

- While standardized tests certainly do inform important decision makers, it is those day-to-day classroom assessments that have the power to meet the information needs of students, teachers, and parents. Standardized tests make only a portion of the total contribution needed to improve our schools.

Chapter 6

Communicating About Student Learning

"So, what did you do in school today?" No doubt this question serves as the most frequently used strategy to find out what's going on in the educational lives of our children. We may be able to focus the question more sharply simply by changing the word "do" to "learn," greatly reducing the probability that we will hear about mixing chocolate milk and lime Jell-O® at lunch. Although what she did at school is important to us, we'd also like to hear from our child what she learned.

Asking the question in either form is our best shot at keeping up with the content and quality of our children's school experiences. The question also illustrates an important component of learning, one that if unrecognized, can result in lower levels of achievement: students have the ability to communicate to us exactly what they are learning, what their successes have been, and what their next steps will be. True, they may need some coaching and practice in learning how to communicate this effectively. But the research is clear; when students are taught to self-assess and to communicate their progress to interested adults, they learn more. This example of direct student involvement in communicating about learning is one of the principles of assessment *for* learning that classroom teachers can build into their teaching routines.

The Primary Purpose

At this point in the book it won't surprise you when we say that we think that the primary (but not the only) reason for communicating about student progress and assessment results ought to be to help students improve their own learning. Therefore, information about student learning should be timely, understandable to both students and parents, and comprised of specific details that describe student progress toward district or state standards. All too frequently, the only communication we get comes in the form of a test score or a report card grade, neither of which provides us or our children with adequate information about what they have learned or still need to learn in a subject. Further, when large-scale standardized test scores are communicated to the public and parents, they rarely appear in the context of helping students learn. In this chapter we'll explore grading and reporting practices that are fundamental to accurate communication and that also promote learning. We'll also suggest strategies parents can use to make sense of assessment results from large-scale standardized tests.

What's in a Grade?

Let's start with report cards and grades. They are a part of the tradition of our school culture and of our larger society. In addition to their role in communication, in the minds of many they represent the rewards and punishments that motivate students. Because of the importance attached to them, they deserve special attention in our examination of school assessment practices. Along the way, it is critical to keep in mind that the grades teachers assign are only as sound as the underlying assessments used to gather the achievement information. If the achievement targets are unclear or the assessments

are of poor quality, then the resulting grades will not accurately reflect your child's learning. If we are to trust that grades mean something, they must be based on accurate assessments.

The Meaning of the Symbol

What does a grade of "C" mean to you? To your child? To your child's teacher? Is a "C" in one classroom equivalent to a "C" in another down the hall? Who else sees the report card? What do the grades mean to them? Grades act as communication symbols from message sender, the teacher, to message receivers, the student and parents, and sometimes to others. Accurate communication relies on the symbols having the same meaning at both ends. This applies not only to a grade of "C" on a report card, but also to terms now commonly used on district and state-level tests and on some school report cards. A student may get a score or a grade indicating he is "proficient" in math, or that she is "emerging" in reading, or "advanced" in writing. Without clear understanding of what those terms mean, we know little about students' achievement levels.

What Goes into the Grade?

A grade of "C" often does not mean the same thing from classroom to classroom, because educators often disagree on what factors should contribute to determining a report card grade. This is a topic that provokes intense discussion among educators and parents. A few examples will show how sticky this issue can be.

Should student performance on homework be considered in the report card grade? If it is, and a student doesn't complete it or turn it in, then the report card grade is lowered. Yet, what if that same student still does extremely well on tests, demonstrating a very high level of achievement? Which is the most accurate communication about achievement, a grade based on test scores or a grade lowered due to missing homework?

Should effort be considered in a final grade? Isn't it important for parents to know how hard their children are trying to learn? But what if the student doesn't need to try hard to learn a great deal? What if it's easy? Should the student receive a lower grade?

What about citizenship and classroom behavior? To get an "A" in mathematics, should it be a requirement that students behave appropriately at all times and model the deportment and responsibility we like to see in all students?

Should attendance count in the grade? If students have poor attendance, it can adversely affect their learning. But should they be encouraged to attend regularly by having attendance be reflected in the final grade? What about being late for class? Should excessive tardiness be factored into a final grade in geometry, for example?

There are good arguments for including each of these factors, and others as well, in the subject-area report card grade. Foremost is the argument that we value these qualities and behaviors. Students need them to do well in school and in life beyond school. We want to send the message that they are important and we want to be able to report how students are doing in these areas as well. Secondary is the argument that if we don't include them in the grade, students won't exhibit these desired characteristics. We want to use grades as motivators to establish habits we believe are important.

There are, however, better reasons for not including habits and behaviors into the report card grade. When anything other than *level of achievement on the stated learning expectations* is figured into a subject-area grade, we lose the meaning of the grade. When other factors are woven in to a grade, we have no way of knowing the extent to which the grade represents a student's level of learning of the subject. If teachers include different factors in report card grades, define them differently, and assess and weight them in different ways, our simple and traditional "A through F" communication system will not convey consistent meaning. Grades must stand alone as symbols with shared meaning between sender and receiver: only when they represent achievement will grades mean the same thing from class to class, and school to school. Therefore we recommend including in the subject-area grade *only* information about level of achievement on the stated learning targets.

A commonsense solution to the desire to communicate about valued habits and behaviors at reporting time is to have a separate place on the report card to do so. This way, if your child gets a "C" in science, you will not have to guess whether it was due to work habits, attitude, or level of understanding

of science concepts. If the habits and behaviors are important enough to gather data about, the report card should be able to communicate clearly about them.

The motivation issue is a bit trickier to solve. Altering a report card grade to reward or punish a student for attitudes and behaviors is not the most effective way to deal with these kinds of problems, and it also causes confusion as to the grade's meaning. There are more effective approaches to solving the complexities of attitude, attendance, and effort problems than using a grade as a stick or a carrot, such as the formative assessment practices described in Chapter 2. No research we know of supports using report card grades to *change* attitude, attendance, or effort. Schools are justified in reporting on them separately, but they are not justified in fiddling with the grade in hopes of changing behaviors.

A further thought about homework and grading: Remember from Chapter 4 that homework can be assigned for different purposes. If the purpose is for practice, descriptive feedback, rather than a grade, is more useful to the student.

Figure 6.1 illustrates a model used to separate out the variables that should be included in the subject-area grade from those variables that are important to report elsewhere.

Not all schools adhere to the principle of including only information about learning in subject-area grades. It is important to

Figure 6.1 Variables Appropriate for Reporting and for Grading

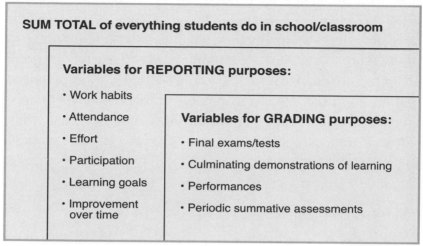

Source: Adapted from "Guidelines for Grading That Support Learning and Student Success" by K. O'Connor, 1995, *NASSP Bulletin, 79* (571), pp. 91–101. Copyright 1995 by NASSP. Adapted by permission. For more information concerning NASSP services and/or programs, please call 703-860-0200, or visit www.principals.org.

ask our child's teacher what is being factored into the report card grade, if it is not clearly stated on the report card or elsewhere. Only then can we interpret grades accurately and know how to support our child's learning.

Computerized Grading Programs

There is one final issue related to grading that we want to address. As described by Guskey (2002a), many teachers today, mostly in secondary schools rather than elementary schools, use a computerized grading program to determine students' grades. These software programs greatly ease teachers' record-keeping chores. Although they mathematically compute grades quickly and efficiently, some grading programs are set up to grade students contrary to what is fair or accurate. For example, they may automatically include zeros in the grade calculation, or rely solely on averaging all of the entered scores to determine the final grade, or include some other variable in the final grade that is not directly related to student learning. They can give the illusion of accuracy and fairness when in reality accuracy and fairness are not there. The decisions about what goes into the grade should come from what we know about sound grading practices, and not from the mind of a computer programmer. Therefore, teachers, students, and parents need to recognize that, while software grading programs can save time, we can't rely on them to do the thinking for us.

The Grading Plan

Just as schools need to communicate *with* us about student learning, they also need to communicate *to* us about how they will arrive at their decisions. Teachers commonly provide students and parents with a written description of learning expectations (sometimes called a *syllabus*) during the first week of the school year. At that time teachers also should explain what they will grade, showing how they will summarize and transform periodic assessments into report card grades. This is often called a *grading plan*. Discussing the grading plan with students at the beginning of instruction is a practice we as parents can look for in our children's classrooms.

Beyond Letter Grades and Symbols

Although a grade can be an informative overall summary of how well a student is doing in a subject, it's the detail—specifically what a student is good at and needs to work on next—that contributes to further learning. Therefore, teachers have developed ways to provide the details we need to help our children learn. These more helpful forms of communication include the following:

- *Checklists of content standards* the student has and has not yet met. These checklists are most helpful if they are broken down into specific learning targets.

- *Developmental continua.* Think about the stages students go through in learning to read. They realize that written words have the same meaning each time they are read, recognize the alphabet, progress to associating sounds with letters and words, and so forth. This developmental sequence, called a *developmental continuum*, can be written out so that teachers, students, and parents can all track progress in a student's learning.

- *Written comments and descriptions of student progress* toward the content standards (sometimes called *anecdotal records*). In this case, teachers note regularly what they see each student succeeding and struggling with. Many primary teachers use anecdotal records to help them keep track of what they need to teach each student. They often share observations from anecdotal records at conference time.

- *Portfolios or other collections of student work.* A *portfolio* is a collection of student work that shows student growth on particular learning targets over a specified time. A writing teacher, for example, might ask students to assemble a portfolio for an English class that contains

  1. Samples of different kinds of writing (a story, a description, an informative report, a persuasive letter)

  2. An explanation of why each piece was chosen—how each displays the characteristics of good writing

  3. A final self-reflection on how their writing has improved over time and what their goals are for future work

117

- *Conferences of various formats, some involving students.* In student-involved conferences, students are responsible for collecting samples of their work in one or more subject areas, and explaining to their parents how these work samples demonstrate what they have learned. In this context, parent, teacher, and student jointly set goals for the next steps in the student's learning.

- *Showcases and fairs.* Many schools host science or math fairs, writing showcases, or history day celebrations to provide an opportunity for students to show what they have been learning. These showcases and fairs offer an opportunity for parents, grandparents, other relatives, and interested community members to find out more about what's going on in their local school.

Finally, many schools recently have redesigned their report cards so that the information they contain reflects state standards and/or district curricula, in an effort to provide students and parents detailed information about student progress relative to these standards. When students communicate about their own progress, they often do so using the standards-based phrases contained in these locally developed report cards.

Students as Communicators

In some school settings, students are passive recipients of information about their learning, rather than engaged information users. One practice that is critical to motivating students to take more responsibility for their learning is to involve them in communicating about their progress and status as learners.

Through self-assessment activities, students develop insight into their own learning. When they inform their teachers and us, their parents, about their learning—the logical next step—they develop pride in their efforts and achievement. The act of communicating what they know about their learning to someone else helps students realize more fully just what they *have* learned. In this context, it is true that nothing succeeds like success. When we know we have done something well, we feel good about our accomplishment and we accept further challenges more enthusiastically. Subsequent learning becomes easier and more enjoyable.

What does this look like? It can take many forms:

- *Samples*: Students bring home samples of their work and talk about them, explaining in detail the specific learning they demonstrate.

- *Notes home*: Students write a note to their parents, telling them how to help them with an assignment ("Dear Mom, please help me revise the organization of my report. Here's how . . . ").

- *Portfolio afternoon*: Students invite friends and relatives to their school's "portfolio afternoons," where they show their work and explain the learning it demonstrates.

- *Showcases or fairs*: Students invite friends and relatives to their school's showcases or fairs, where they show their work and explain the learning it demonstrates.

- *Conferences*: Students take part in or lead a conference with their teacher and parents to examine their work, discuss strengths, and identify new goals for learning.

- *Exit exhibitions or senior projects*: High school students prepare and present a demonstration of learning in a variety of subject areas.

Communication About Standardized Tests

Over the last 10 years, most states, districts, and schools have faced an added communication challenge of describing to parents and the public the new tests they have adopted or that their state accountability legislation has required. Explaining what types of items appear on the tests, how they are scored, what they measure, what the results mean, how the results will and won't be used, the amount of time spent testing, and costs to the taxpayer keeps school officials busy.

Just as a grade of "C" might not mean the same from one classroom or school to the next, the definition of what it means to be "proficient" on one state's standardized test may not equate to the definition on another state's test. It is important to keep in mind that even though districts and states have developed content standards to guide teaching and learning, these learning expectations do vary, both in number of expectations and in level of difficulty. Some contain lots of smaller content standards; others contain fewer, more comprehensive content standards. Some present ambitious learning goals for students, reflecting what students should be capable of when the standards are fully implemented over a period of years; others identify learning goals students are more easily able to attain during the current school term.

So, we have to inquire about the rigor of our state and district content standards. In addition, we must recognize that the definition of "how good is good enough" will not be the same from state to state or district to district. This definition, called the *performance standard*, is not a statement of the learning; rather it is a statement of the level of acceptable quality. The example we are most familiar with in the classroom context is the "passing grade." In many schools today, the passing grade—the performance standard—is still a "D-minus." A grade of "D-minus," although not likely to open doors for high school graduates in the same way an "A" grade will, still constitutes a passing grade, and is therefore "good enough" for some students as well as for some school systems.

Unfortunately, it is often the case that score reports on state-level tests include little specific information for parents to judge how well their children are learning, and the reports can be hard to read, as well. To communicate clearly to parents and the community about standardized tests, we recommend that every school prepare answers to the following questions:

- Why is this test being given to students? The answer should contain a brief description of the test and a list of intended uses of the results.

- What content does this test measure? The content should directly relate to the district curriculum.

- Is the test timed? How long will it take?

- What assessment methods are used on the test?

121

- How will the results be reported? Will the information come back as a percentile score? Will it reflect the student's proximity to the performance standard? Will the score reflect a grade-level equivalent? Will the data show what students know relative to specific learning expectations?

- If the score comes back as a reference to the performance standard, what does it mean to "be proficient," or to have "met the standard?" What do the terms mean? All terminology in the score report should be clearly explained.

- What strategies can we parents use after we get the results to help our children take the next steps in their learning?

- Whom should parents or community members contact for more information?

The following kinds of communications may also be available from our schools or districts:

- A set of frequently asked questions about testing, the content standards the test measures, and the accountability system it serves

- A fact sheet about the test itself

- A parent handbook on content standards and assessment

- A glossary of assessment and testing terms

- Sample student score reports with interpretive guides

- Sample test items with examples of scored student responses

- Videotapes produced by the state or district to inform the public about the testing program

- Tips on how parents can help prepare students to do their best on district or state tests

Reconciling State Test Results to Report Card Grades

Earlier we referred to the fact that the level of rigor on state tests varies widely, as does the performance standard. In one state, 70 percent of fourth graders may meet the standard on the mathematics test, while in another only 20 percent may meet the standard. As we have seen, we must be careful in interpreting the meaning of these two scores; one state may or may not be doing a better job of educating children. It might be that the test is harder in one state. The test might be scored more strictly in one state. Or, students might be expected to know more in one state than another.

This issue serves to illustrate another problem, one we may more commonly experience: an apparent mismatch between state test results and report card grades. A state test may indicate that a student has not met the reading standard. Yet the student's report card grade in reading may be a "B." Adding confusion may be a score on an earlier test indicating the student is reading at or above grade level. How can a state test report overall weakness when the student is receiving a grade of "B" and glowing comments from the classroom teacher? Can the performance standard held by the classroom teacher and the performance standard held by the state for the annual test be so different?

Such mismatches do occur. Possible causes include a lack of alignment between what your child learned in the classroom and what was tested, faulty classroom grading practices, a problem in the testing situation that day, or a problem your child was having on the day of the test. While some possible causes might lead you to disregard the test results, you need to make sure you understand the source of the discrepancy before concluding that the test scores are inaccurate. If you find yourself in this situation, don't ignore it. We recommend that you schedule a conversation with  your child's teacher, using the following questions, among others you may have, as a guide:

1. Can you help me understand how the grade that you assigned accurately reflects my child's achievement?

2. What achievement targets did you teach and assess in the classroom?

3. What academic standards are tested by the state? How do those relate to your classroom achievement targets?

4. Are your tests and the state assessment measuring the same things? If not, what are the differences?

5. How did the state assess the content standards? Is it possible the state assessment is not an accurate reflection of my child's achievement?

In the answers to these questions you may discover similarities and differences in achievement expectations, assessment processes, performance standards, and the meaning of the results. You may also gain insight into your child as a learner. It is important to keep in mind that the impetus for such conversations is your child's well-being. It will be helpful to keep the conversation focused on how you and the teacher can use assessment results to promote your child's academic achievement.

Chapter 6 — Important Ideas

- There is no single best way to deliver messages about student achievement. Grades meet some needs some of the time, but cannot hope to serve all information needs.

- The basic principles of sound report card grading should be reflected in district grading policies as well as in the classroom. We can ask key questions to see if they are present.

- Report card grades in each subject area should provide us a clear and untainted indication of the student's current level of achievement. If schools have quality information about other factors such as effort, attendance, and citizenship to report, they should appear separately on the report card.

- Students have a key role to play in communicating about their learning, and the acts of preparing for and carrying out that role can increase their learning and their motivation to learn.

- Judging the quality of schools and evaluating the learning of individual students carry the same caution: giving too much attention to any one single achievement indicator can skew the picture of group or individual progress.

Chapter 7

Putting the Pieces Together:
Parent and Community Involvement
in School Assessment

Promoting the learning and protecting the well-being of our children is at the center of the work we do as parents and educators. In those efforts we join every other parent and teacher and the countless thousands of citizens across the country with an active interest in the education of children and the quality of schools. Now more than ever, during this era of increased student testing we think parents should not automatically assume that students are being accurately assessed, either in the classroom or on state tests.

In this final chapter we'll review some of the key points we've presented in earlier chapters and link those summaries with your role as a parent or interested community member. For each of the six previous chapters we'll offer questions you can ask of your local educators to help inform yourself about the issues at hand and the assessment climate in local schools and classrooms. We also suggest specific things you can look for relative to issues of assessment quality, balance, and purpose.

At the classroom level, because we know that the majority of the nation's teachers have not been required to be certified as competent assessors of student learning, many may not be trained or effective in that role. That does not mean high-quality classroom assessment isn't happening in many classrooms or can't happen in most. It does mean, however, that parents should have a level of curiosity about all forms of assessment.

As for the large-scale assessments *of* learning your children take, we encourage you as parents to ask the school questions about these tests, how and why they are used, their results, and what they mean and don't mean (National Education Association 2002):

- Are there any differences between the mandated state tests and other district or national standardized tests given? Do they assess the same things?

- How are students being prepared for all of the standardized tests they take? How much time is that taking, and is learning in subjects not tested affected adversely?

- Is a single test score being used to make any decisions about students?

By doing this you can begin to learn if students are being over-tested or if tests are mismatched to the intended purpose. And by inquiring about both assessments *of* and *for* learning, you can verify that powerful learning opportunities are at work in the classroom, benefiting all students.

Working with the Schools

Our purpose is to leave you with a sense of having the ability to take whatever steps you see as appropriate to promote learning and advocate for quality in your local schools using assessment as the vehicle. It is important to keep in mind that we do not believe our job or yours as a parent or community member is to "fix" whatever assessment problems you might encounter. Instead, our hope is that teachers and principals can count on us as allies, partners to work with in advocating for best practice in assessment for the sake of all students. When we help districts or schools find solutions to the issues they face we accomplish this goal. To do this effectively requires that we place a high value on the relationship between us as parents and the school, a relationship that if spoiled is likely to end any opportunity for improvement. Keep in mind the following to help maintain a healthy, working relationship with schools and teachers:

- Focus on building the partnership through a relationship based on mutual respect; teachers and administrators also have student well-being at heart.

- Reinforce the positive, helping to sustain what is already in place and working well.

- Gather as much pertinent data and information as possible, asking clarifying questions along the way.

- Share ideas in a spirit of helping, and be willing to hear ideas on how you can help.

- Communicate regularly during the year on a variety of topics. This helps establish a relationship of trust, keeps communication channels open, and increases receptivity in times of problem solving.

What Parents Should Know and Can Do

Chapter 1: Assessment in Schools Today

Our state and local assessment systems will truly serve student learning when we blend and balance high-quality standardized testing programs, assessments *of* learning, with high-quality classroom assessment *for* learning. This balance has traditionally been absent in most schools but must be present if students are to meet high standards. To learn about the balance that exists in your school and district, consider finding the answers to some or all of the following questions (Stiggins & Knight 1997):

- Does your school or district have a plan that addresses the need for balanced assessment systems? Is there a philosophy of assessment and a school board policy that supports that balance?

- Is there a vision of what high-quality assessment consists of? Does it include standards of quality for all assessments? Does it define how classroom assessment fits into the bigger picture of testing in the school, district, and state?

- Is the vision spelled out in a written plan for parents and others to see?

In Chapter 1 we described what we believe is a mismatch between what the public believes about classroom assessment practices in schools and what little opportunity teachers in general have had to become assessment literate. As indicated, many teachers do not yet know the difference between sound and unsound assessment practices; assessment quality and accuracy suffer as a result.

As a parent, it may help you to know what we believe a teacher who is assessment literate knows and is able to do with regard to assessment, so you can watch for those practices in your child's education. The specific knowledge and skills we'd like to see in every teacher include the following:

- Teachers understand and clearly define, in advance of teaching, the achievement targets the students are to hit.

- Teachers inform students regularly, in terms they can understand, about those achievement targets.

- Teachers ensure that students themselves can describe what targets they are to hit and what comes next in their learning.

- Teachers can transform these achievement targets into dependable assessments that yield accurate information.

- Teachers understand the relationship between assessment and student motivation and use assessment to build student confidence.

- Teachers consistently use classroom assessment information to revise instruction.

- Teacher feedback to students is frequent, immediate, and descriptive.

- Teachers intentionally create opportunities for students to be actively involved in their own assessment, including communicating about their own learning to others.

131

In addition, the following strategies can help you determine if the principles of sound assessment practice are at work in your local school:

- Talk to teachers about the assessments they conduct in the classroom. Use the previous list to seek information about the classroom assessment environment.

- Ask the principal if there has been a schoolwide professional development effort in classroom assessment literacy to help teachers acquire this set of knowledge and skills.

- Examine the school's grading policy. See how issues of effort, attendance, and class participation are dealt with. Talk with your child's teachers to see how they deal with the issues of grading and reporting.

- Look at how student progress is communicated: as a single grade, a narrative description, an evaluation of progress vis-à-vis the written curriculum standards. Are there other ways you'd appreciate being informed about your child's progress? If so, discuss those ideas with school personnel. Some of those ideas and options may already exist as school practices.

The Preparation and Support Our Teachers Need

The common myth is that teachers come out of their preparation programs in colleges and universities ready for a lifetime of classroom teaching, needing no further training. The fact is that teaching is no different than other professions where new research can inform new practices, yielding improved results. Staying current with what works and knowing how to implement best practices in the classroom are critical to effective schools. Experts know that nothing is as important to student learning as a knowledgeable, competent teacher.

Professional development—increasing teachers' skills—is the answer to having all classroom teachers become assessment literate so they can apply the principles of assessment *for* learning in their classrooms. It is *the* fundamental ingredient in school improvement. The competition for teachers' professional development time and attention is fierce. Although many industries and companies may invest up to 20 percent or more of their budgets in training and retraining employees, educational systems have little to budget in this area—it is routinely below 5 percent of the total budget, often far below.

To compound the issue, frequently what is available to teachers for their professional growth is offered to them as a menu, accompanied by little information about the impact of each item on student learning to guide their selections. The return on investment for schools and districts can be hard to track. Sometimes, this has led to suspicion regarding teacher professional development and even to direct criticism by those who may view it as an unnecessary frill or as tax money poorly spent.

Certain models for professional development, such as school-based learning teams, have been proven to be more effective than others (American Institute for Research 1999). We encourage parents and community members to view professional development as essential, to learn how local schools and districts are investing in the ongoing development of their teaching staff and what obstacles they might face, and to support effective professional development when it is in place. In doing so, keep in mind these common guidelines for quality:

- Is it organized in study groups inside a school that values collaborative learning, or is its main focus sending individuals to traditional workshops and conferences? Workshops and conferences are a good way to gain new information, but the study group approach is more effective in transferring new ideas into classroom practice.

- Is it ongoing—does it provide continued support beyond a one-time shot at learning something new?

- Is there an emphasis on learning about and applying productive strategies, with opportunities for active learning?

Just as we want quality learning environments for our children, we also desire the same thing for our children's teachers. Schools that model continuous learning for their students by having teachers visibly engaged in learning send a message to students and the community about learning being a lifelong process.

Chapter 2: Connecting Student Motivation and Assessment

Student involvement in classroom assessment can have a major impact on student motivation to learn and on learning itself. When students want to learn it is because they feel capable of learning, and high-quality formative assessment in the class-room can breed confidence and genuine success. This is not about building self-esteem; it is about using academic success to raise the confidence of students and to lead them to become better learners. From this, natural self-esteem and motivation will follow.

Students engage in assessment *for* learning when they use assessment information to set goals or make learning decisions related to their own improvement, or communicate about their status and progress toward established learning goals. Students are involved in their own assessment if they are working with their teacher to do the following:

- Understand the attributes of good performance.

- Use scoring criteria and rubrics to evaluate the quality of anonymous work.

- Evaluate the quality of their own work: identify areas of strength and set goals for improvement.

- Create draft test "blueprints" and/or practice tests based on their understanding of the learning targets they are to hit and the essential concepts in the material they are to learn.

135

- Talk with others about their growth and identify when they are getting close to success.

- Accumulate evidence of their own improvement in growth portfolios.

- Lead or participate in parent–teacher conferences.

- Plan their next steps for learning.

We know that students regularly receive judgmental feedback in forms other than grades or critical comments. "You really tried hard on this one," "You really did great," or a smiley face sticker at the top of the page seem to many parents and even educators normal and acceptable. It is all well intended, to be sure, but it doesn't conform with what we know works. If only judgmental feedback is given the majority of the time, teachers miss a huge opportunity to help students learn. Students need information on which to revise and improve future work. Carefully delivered descriptive feedback is one of the most important and useful sources of information for both you and your child about how he or she is doing in school. As a parent you can look for the following:

- Descriptive communication to your child about the strengths of her or his work

- Understandable descriptions about why an answer is correct or incorrect

- Clear, constructive suggestions on how your child can improve

- Examples of quality work that provide a model of excellence to strive toward, with explanations of the elements of quality

If you do not understand the marks or comments from the teacher, ask your child to explain them. If your child cannot, or if the explanation does not make sense to you, contact your child's teacher.

Chapter 3: What Students Learn: Standards, Curriculum, and Learning Targets

During the last decade, states and districts have developed academic content standards for most grades and subjects, with tests now in place to measure student progress toward those standards. In many schools the standards are rigorous, and some students initially will have difficulty meeting them. Following are suggestions for how you as parents can learn what the standards look like in your local school:

- See if there is a written curriculum in your school by grade and/or by subject. Many districts and states have these documents posted on the Internet. Is it connected grade level to grade level? Do teachers use it as a means to communicate expectations, guide instruction, and report student progress?

- Print (or request) copies of the content standards and grade-level curriculum and keep them on file so you can refer to them at home during the school year. Also, use them to become familiar with what is expected of your child grade by grade. We taped our daughter's grade-level expectations to the refrigerator door, and she often referred to them to gauge her own progress.

When teachers make the learning target clear to students for each and every lesson and relate that learning to what came before and what follows, the probability of learning increases.

Further, if students know why the learning is important, and they know what successful, quality learning looks like in each instance, learning improves. As a parent, you can help:

- Ask your children if their learning targets are clear to them each day.

- Ask them if they know why they are learning what they are learning and how it may help them in the future, connecting it to life beyond school. If they cannot explain this, discuss with the teacher how she informs students about classroom learning expectations.

- Look at the assessments your child brings home. Look for these connections: Does what is being assessed match what is being taught, and does that match the written curriculum?

- Monitor the balance of the learning targets your child is expected to master: knowledge, reasoning, performance, and products. Use Tables 3.2 and 4.1 to help you determine the balance of assessment methods you might expect to see.

Chapter 4: Classroom Assessment: Principles, Methods, and Issues of Quality

In every instance the *method* used to assess should be a match for the type of *learning target* being assessed. For example, we've traditionally assessed writing in this country using multiple-choice questions about the rules of grammar. It's become clear that some students can do well on that kind of test but in reality cannot write clearly or succinctly. Measuring knowledge about the structure of language or the conventions of writing (capitalization, parts of speech, punctuation, etc.) using a selected response test is fine. But if we want to know how well students

can apply those rules and how clearly they write, we must sample their writing with essay or performance assessment.

Teachers who are competent assessors of student learning have the following knowledge and skills relating to assessment methods and standards of quality. You can look for these in your child's classroom and/or talk with the teacher about how these skills are at work for your child.

Purpose

- Teachers know why they are giving the assessment and how the information will be used.

- They have chosen the kind of assessment they will use with the purpose in mind.

- They conduct a variety of assessments to meet the information needs of all those whose decisions affect students' well-being.

- Students in their classes can explain why they are taking the assessment and how the information will be used.

- Students' information needs are met, and they receive timely, accurate feedback about their learning in a way that encourages them to keep going.

Targets

- Teachers can explain the specific learning targets they are teaching and measuring.

- Students in their classes also can state what those targets are.

- The specific learning targets come from a carefully planned sequence for learning created at the local (school district) level, and representing current knowledge about what students need to know and be able to do when they graduate.

Methods

- Teachers use a variety of assessment methods, determined by the kind of learning targets they are assessing and the purposes for the assessment.

- They are able to use each assessment method accurately and efficiently.

- Teachers who use homework as an assessment tool understand that not all homework is created equal. They can explain the homework's purpose, and can tell you what forms of parent involvement with it will maximize your child's learning.

Chapter 5: Standardized Testing

All large-scale statewide tests aren't created equal. Some simply are better than others. In judging the quality of the statewide test administered in your district it's helpful to know the answers to the following questions:

1. Are the results of the state test reported back to students and parents standard by standard? If scores are combined into one score or reported by percentiles, little information is available about student mastery of and progress toward the state standards. Is a report included that shares specific strengths and weaknesses for your child?

2. Is the test timed, requiring students to finish in one sitting, or does it allow students to work until they have completed the assessment? If students don't have to beat the clock, an unspoken message is sent that we value their best work and sincere effort, that quality counts, and that they needn't race through the test to be sure they finish.

Just as college admissions offices are expanding entry criteria beyond the traditional admissions test score to include samples of student writing and other predictors of probable success, we need to view school effectiveness the same way. The quality of the environment your child is in, how well the school focuses on and nurtures learning, and how well it motivates children to want to learn are as important as any score that might also be representative of the school academic program.

Schools have a wealth of information they can share about overall school quality and performance, and the performance of individual students. But everything that is important about a student or a school cannot be summarized in a single test score. The paper-and-pencil norm-referenced tests are fine for specific purposes, but they do not and cannot measure everything of importance. Further, by themselves they are inadequate measures of overall school quality and effectiveness. What measures of success does your school or district use to hold itself accountable for the large portion of valued learning not measured by norm-referenced tests? How are these measures consistent with your child's results on other assessments? Is there a pattern?

Chapter 6: Communicating About Student Learning

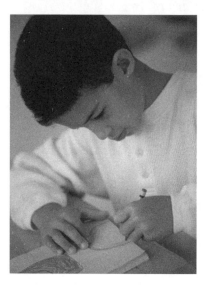

Communicating about student progress should not be a one-time event. Rather, it should be viewed as a continuous process that provides timely information in a variety of ways about what students are learning and how well they are learning it. To be effective, teacher, parent, and student must share understanding about the content of the message and any symbols that may be used as part of that message.

Assessment information coming home can include student input, journals, self-assessment results, portfolios, student growth plans, and suggestions for home support as well as test scores and report card grades. Effective communication uses the defined learning expectations and criteria for assessment as the foundation for the message. In other words, school reports to parents about how well students are doing communicate directly and in understandable terms about what students are expected to know and do.

Many schools have adopted report cards that are linked to state standards and/or district curriculum expectations, thereby providing information on student progress relative to those standards. In this case make sure that you do the following (Dietel 2001):

1. Understand clearly the terms used on the report. Look at the report card before it comes out, and if the terms are not clear, talk with the teacher.

2. Talk with your child about the content/format/terms on the report card, making sure it is clear to her.

3. Ask your child to rate himself using the terms and see how that compares to those given by the teacher.

4. Ask your child if she knows what to do to improve in areas showing need.

Allowing students to track their own progress as learners and then communicate that progress to others is a way for students to be involved in assessment itself, a key principle of assessment *for* learning. If scoring rubrics are used by the district/state, keep copies available at home. It is essential to understand what factors do and do not go into calculating the report card grade and to understand clearly what the symbols (grades, letters, numbers, etc.) mean in terms of what your child has learned. Look for a variety of tools and strategies used by the school to communicate about student achievement, and ask your child if he or she can explain how grades are determined. Keep a file of all assessment results that come home.

Remember that the full picture of student learning, including the specific strengths and weaknesses of each learner, is portrayed more accurately through multiple sources of information than by a single grade or score. Look for state and district individual student score reports that describe the test, explain the results, and when appropriate, describe the proficiency levels required to "pass" the test in user-friendly terms.

Conclusion

Just as the research is clear regarding the gains that can be realized in student achievement when the principles of assessment *for* learning are applied in the classroom, it is also clear that parental involvement has a positive effect on student learning. More and more schools and districts have recognized that, as described in the research and carried out in high-performing schools, parental involvement can lead to reduced dropout rates, higher graduation rates, and improved student performance. Many schools and districts now welcome parent involvement and structure policies, procedures, and activities to support and encourage it. They develop resources for parents to use at home, parent guides to the curriculum, sample assessments and test questions, and tips on helping their children in every subject area.

As parents, we need to recognize the value of our involvement in the educational lives of our children and take advantage of the opportunities many schools afford in this area. Involvement can come in many forms—in this book we've encouraged involvement through knowledge of effective classroom assessment and by providing ideas for what parents can do to ensure healthy classroom assessment practices for their children. We hope that you parents who read this book will be better able to do the following:

- Understand the information about student achievement coming home and know where it fits into the big picture.

- Monitor your child's learning through teacher feedback.

- Encourage your children to set their own goals for learning using feedback on previous work.

- Know when to worry, when to monitor more closely, and what to celebrate.

- Know why your child is doing each assignment and how the work relates to the learning targets for the class.

- Know how to help your child at home.

Away from the school and the classroom, we believe that anyone who desires to can provide leadership and direction in assessment policy, at the local, state, or federal level. Many community members do not have children in schools, but do pay taxes, care about the education our young people are receiving, and worry that America is reported to be far behind other countries in some areas of education. Policy makers need to hear parents, teachers, and community members advocating for balanced assessment systems, for increased allocation of resources for professional development in classroom assessment, and for the appropriate use of large-scale tests.

We know schools and teachers today are enormously challenged, criticized at far too many turns. Often, test results are used for political purposes while real, valid indicators of student learning and school quality and effectiveness are ignored. School principals face more than they should ever have to; the number of applicants for administrative positions continues to decline as the enormity of the task grows. And in the classroom, teachers face challenges that those not in the classroom do not fully understand. The looming teacher shortage may indicate that these challenges are increasing in complexity. And adding to the already difficult conditions are educational funding systems that vary widely in their levels of adequacy, not only state to state, but even district to district.

There are many obstacles to improved schools. Yet, we know that many schools have successfully leapt those hurdles and now serve students as individuals, taking all from where they are now in their learning and helping them progress to where they need to be. In doing so, educators have recognized that assessment can do far more than measure how much learning has occurred. It serves us best not as a source of pressure to improve schools through public accountability; assessment can serve as the cause of student and school success. School environments in which this is happening encourage learning and build confidence.

All of our nation's students can be, and deserve the chance to be, successful learners. We hope for every child what we want for our own child's schooling: a focus on learning, classrooms with caring and competent teachers, and a school environment that nurtures students individually—physically, academically, and emotionally. We know that as parents we have a responsibility not only in sending our daughter to school ready to learn, but also in advocating for the school environment we describe in this book. We welcome those responsibilities. We know there are many others, just like us, who appreciate the privilege and opportunity given to every citizen in this country to make meaningful contributions to education in whatever ways possible. We do this for all our children.

Glossary of Assessment Terms

Accountability

Student performance on assessments linked to content standards that lead to rewards or consequences for schools and sometimes educators. Large-scale standardized tests are used to collect the information used for accountability decisions.

Assessment

The process of gathering information about student achievement, most often in relation to defined learning expectations. Using a variety of methods can provide information to a variety of users for a variety of decisions.

Assessment literacy

The term used to describe the set of knowledge and skills educators need to gather accurate and reliable information about student learning and to be able to use that information in productive ways.

Assessment methods

The different ways used in schools to evaluate learning. There are four basic categories of assessment methods: *selected response, essay, performance assessment,* and *personal communication.*

Bias

A lack of objectivity or fairness, used in this case to describe a potential problem in student assessment.

Content standards

The broadest, most general form of learning expectation from which more specific grade-level curriculum is derived. Content standards exist for most states in most subjects, describing what students should know and be able to do.

Criterion-referenced test

An assessment that measures student progress toward specific curriculum goals or standards. Scores are reported in comparison to a predefined acceptable level of performance rather than in comparison to other students.

Curriculum

A more specific version of the *content standards*, usually designed for each subject area at an individual grade level. Curriculum guides what is taught in the classroom. It is a collection of statements of the objectives, or learning goals, to be taught in each subject.

Curriculum objective

A specific learning goal to be taught in a specific subject. See *curriculum*.

Descriptive feedback

Information related to the assigned learning task and provided to students to help them take the next steps in their learning by showing them what they already do well, what they need to improve, and how.

Essay questions

A method of assessment designed to measure students' knowledge and reasoning proficiencies. To perform well on an essay test question, students must answer the question asked and provide the information required.

Evaluation

The process of collecting information from multiple sources to make judgments (assign a grade, for example) about how well students have learned.

Evaluative feedback

Feedback that tells learners how they compare to others or that provides a judgment summarizing the quality of the learning. Letter grades, numbers, symbols, and written phrases are typically used to deliver this type of feedback.

Extrinsic motivation

Motivation deriving from external sources, such as promise of reward or threat of punishment.

Formative assessment

Purposeful, ongoing collection of information about how students are learning while there is still time to improve. Both teacher and student then use the information to guide continuous improvement toward the intended learning.

Grade

A letter, number, or other symbol assigned to summarize the quality of student performance.

Grading

The process of assigning letters or numbers at the end of a period of time (term, semester, etc.) as a way to summarize the quality of student performance.

Grade-level equivalent score

A score that corresponds to chronological age and grade in school. A student scoring at 5.3, no matter what age, would be interpreted as scoring the average for a student in the third month of fifth grade.

High-stakes testing

Tests that have important decisions about students, teachers, and schools tied to the results. For students this could mean a decision regarding promotion or retention, mandatory course selections, or even graduation. For schools not attaining expected achievement levels, typical consequences include the withholding of funds, teacher or principal reassignment, school reorganization, or in some cases, school closure.

Intrinsic motivation

Motivation deriving from internal sources, such as satisfaction in accomplishment or pleasure in an activity.

Large-scale assessment

Assessments in which large numbers of students participate and from which systemwide (district, state, etc.) data are collected, often for accountability purposes.

Learning targets

These are the most specific forms of learning expectations that define the objectives of daily lessons. They are the smaller, teachable and assessable parts of learning that make up the larger whole of curriculum objectives. Learning targets for individual lessons underpin and support the content standard, leading students to where they are ready to demonstrate that they can meet the standard.

Multiple measures

Using information about student learning from a variety of sources and in a variety of ways to inform decision making.

Norm-referenced test

A test, often one of basic skills and concepts, developed to measure one student's performance against the performance of other students of the same age and/or grade who have previously taken the same test.

Percentile

The score used most frequently to report individual student results on norm-referenced tests. A score at the 63rd percentile means that student scored as high or better than 63 percent of the norm group, the students who originally took the test.

Performance assessment

An assessment that requires the student to construct a response, create a product, or perform a demonstration. Evaluation of the knowledge and/or skills displayed is based on observation and judgment with the help of scoring criteria.

Performance criteria

The description of quality that students are to aim for in a performance assessment.

Performance tasks

The assignment in a performance assessment.

Performance standard

The predetermined level of acceptable performance on an assessment, answering the question, "How good is good enough?"

Personal communication

An assessment method in which the teacher asks a question or engages in a dialogue with the student, and listens to determine the quality of the response. Assessments in the primary grades rely heavily on this one-on-one method.

Portfolio

A collection of student work that reflects student progress toward the intended learning.

Rubric

A scoring tool or set of criteria used to evaluate student performance on a task or test.

Sampling

Reliable assessments need to gather the right amount of information about the learning to be measured. Does the assessor have enough information to draw confident conclusions about students' achievement on each of the content standards? How much information is enough? These issues of sampling need to be considered in the design of any assessment.

Scoring guide

See *rubric*.

Self-assessment

A process in which students collect information about their own learning, analyze what it reveals about their progress toward the intended learning goals, and plan the next steps in their learning.

Selected response tests

Tests used to measure students' knowledge and reasoning proficiencies. They have one correct answer or a limited number of correct answers, and can include multiple-choice, matching, fill-in-the-blank or short answer, and true-false items.

Standardized tests

Tests that are given and scored in exactly the same way for all students. Standardized tests can be either norm or criterion referenced, which refers to how the scores are reported.

Student-involved conference

Communication about student learning in which the student takes an active role in planning and delivering the information, usually to parents or guardians, with the help of the teacher.

Summative assessment

An assessment given in class at the end of a period of study, or an external, standardized test used to summarize what students have learned up to that point. Frequently evaluations of students are made and grades are assigned based on their results.

Bibliography

American Institute for Research. (1999). *Designing effective professional development: Lessons from the Eisenhower program.* Washington, DC: U.S. Department of Education.

Arter, J. A., and Busick, K. U. (2001). *Practice with student-involved classroom assessment.* Portland, OR: Assessment Training Institute.

Assessment Reform Group. (1999). *Assessment for learning: Beyond the black box.* Cambridge, UK: University of Cambridge.

Atkin, J. M., Black, P., and Coffey, J. (2001). *Classroom assessment and the National Science Standards.* Washington, DC: National Academy Press.

Black, P., and Wiliam, D. (1998). Inside the black box: Raising standards through classroom assessment. *Phi Delta Kappan, 80*(2), 139–148.

Burger, D. (1997). *Designing a sustainable standards-based assessment system.* Aurora, CO: Mid-continent Regional Educational Laboratory.

Chappuis, S., and Stiggins, R. J. (2002). Classroom assessment for learning. *Educational Leadership, 60*(1), 40–44.

Clark, S. (2001). *Unlocking formative assessment.* London, UK: Hodder & Stoughton.

Crooks, T. (2001). *The validity of formative assessments.* Leeds, UK: British Educational Research Association.

Davies, A. (2000). *Making classroom assessment work.* Merville, BC: Connections.

Dietel, R. (2001). How is my child doing in school? *Our Children, 26*(6), 6–8.

Falk, B. (2002). Standards-based reforms: Problems and possibilities. *Phi Delta Kappan, 83*(8), 612–620.

Guskey, T. R. (2002a). Computerized gradebooks and the myth of objectivity. *Phi Delta Kappan, 83*(10), 775–780.

Guskey, T. R. (2002b). *How's my kid doing? A parent's guide to grades, marks and report cards*. San Francisco: Jossey-Bass.

Guskey, T. R., and Bailey, J. M. (2001). *Developing grading and reporting systems for student learning*. Thousand Oaks, CA: Corwin.

Lewis, A. (2000). *High-stakes testing: Trends and issues. Policy brief*. Aurora, CO: Mid-continent Regional Educational Laboratory.

McDermott, T. K., and McDermott, D. F. (2002). High-stakes testing for students with special needs. *Phi Delta Kappan, 83*(7), 504–544.

National Education Association. (2002). *Parent's guide to testing and accountability*. Washington, DC: NEA Communications.

O'Connor, K. (2002). *The mindful school: How to grade for learning*. Arlington Heights, IL: Skylight.

Olson, L. (2002a). A "proficient" score depends upon geography. *Education Week, 21*(24), 1–6.

Olson, L. (2002b). Forum bemoans gap between standards and classroom. *Education Week, 21*(29), 14–15.

Petersen, S., and Shutes, R. (1994). Seven reasons why text-books cannot make a curriculum. *NASSP Bulletin, 78*(565), 11–20.

Popham, W. J. (2001). *The truth about testing: An educator's call to action*. Alexandria, VA: ASCD.

Sadler, R. (1989). Formative assessment and the design of instructional systems. *Instructional Science, 18,* 119–144.

Schmoker, M. (2002). The real causes of higher achievement. *SEDLetter, 14*(2). Retrieved July 2002 from the World Wide Web: http://www.sedl.org/pubs/sedletter/v14n02/1.html

Shepard, L. A. (2000). The role of assessment in a learning culture. *Educational Researcher, 29*(7), 4–14.

Shepard, L. A. (2001). Using assessment to help students think about learning. Keynote address at Assessment Training Institute Summer Conference, Portland, OR.

Stiggins, R. J. (1999). Assessment, student confidence, and school success. *Phi Delta Kappan, 81*(3), 191–198.

Stiggins, R. J. (2001). *Student-involved classroom assessment,* 3rd ed. Upper Saddle River, NJ: Merrill-Prentice Hall.

Stiggins, R. J., and Knight, T. (1997). *But are they learning?* Portland, OR: Assessment Training Institute.

Wagner, T. (2002). *Making the grade: Reinventing America's schools*. New York: Routledge Falmer.

York Region District School Board. (2001). *Assessment and evaluation*. The Curriculum Series, vol. 2. Aurora, ON: Author.

About the Authors

Jan Chappuis

Prior to joining ATI, Jan was a school district curriculum and assessment specialist in Washington State as well as a consultant to districts throughout the country. She has over a decade of experience in providing K–12 staff development in assessment designed to improve student achievement. Her classroom background includes 12 years teaching grades 4 through 9. Currently, Jan leads ATI professional development efforts in student-involved assessment strategies, providing teachers and instructional leaders with practical solutions for motivating students and involving them in their own academic success.

Steve Chappuis

Steve's career as a teacher, counselor, and building and district administrator in public school districts in Washington State spans over 28 years. His experiences include serving as a junior high principal, a senior high principal, and assistant superintendent for curriculum and instruction. In the latter role he implemented a standards-based instructional program that included comprehensive assessment plans and policies with professional development for teachers in classroom assessment. As director of ATI's training operations, Steve works with educators and school leaders to develop assessment literacy and balanced local assessment systems.

WITHDRAWN

MAY 0 6 2024

DAVID O. McKAY LIBRARY
BYU-IDAHO